# UNLOCKING GOD'S POWER, FAVOR AND BLESSINGS IN YOUR LIFE

## A NEW APPROACH IN PRAYING AND READING THE SCRIPTURES

*I command every evil plantation with all of its roots, to come out of my body in Jesus name.*

# GILLIAN N. WHYTE

DENVER, COLORADO

## Dedication

*To every person who has a hunger for God's Word, and an unquenchable devotion to, and zeal for, prayer and intercession. Those who hunger and thirst after righteousness shall be filled (Matthew 5: 6). Let these pages fill your heart, mind and soul, and bring you into power, favor and blessings.*

*To my god-children: Joshua, Zayne-Alexis and Danielle; my neices and nephews: Julia, Desroy, Jessica, James, Carrdavia and Gabrielle; may the Wod of God be your inheritance and may its truth be the guiding influence in all your decisions.*

*For as the rain cometh down and the snow from heaven and returns not thither but waters the earth and makes it bring forth and bud, that it may give seed to the sower and bread to the eater; So shall my word be that goes forth out of my mouth: it shall not return unto me void, but it shall accomplish that which I please, and it shall prosper in the thing whereto I sent it."*
*(Isaiah 55:10-11)*

# Contents

**Apocalyptic Book:**

**Bonus Prayers:**

# Acknowledgment

I thank the Heavenly Father and the Holy Spirit for empowering me to conceptualize the prayers in this book.

To all those who supported me through prayer and timely words of encouragement, thank you.

Thanks to the team at Outskirts Press for making this book a reality.

# Foreword

*Unlocking God's Power, Favor and Blessings in your Life,* focuses on how using the Word of God can help to develop a stable life of prayer. Gillian displays how the Scripture is an effective tool for prayer. Coupled with her passion for the Word of God and her insatiable need to pray, she develops prayers that have helped her to grow.

For mature people in Christ, reading *Unlocking God's Power, Favor and Blessings in your Life* will refuel and rekindle a passion for prayer and the Word of God. The young believer in Christ will grow in their depth of God's Word and will learn the power of praying the Scriptures.

Prayer is communicating with God. When we pray the Scriptures, we speak God's words to Him. As you pray the Word of God, He will open your mind to His will; unlocking His power, favor and blessings in your life.

I recommend this book to everyone. If you need to grow in your prayer life or gain a passion for prayer and the Word of God, this book is for you. My own faith grew through diligent study in prayer and reading the Word. Read this book and realize the change that will come to your Christian life.

Rupert Bailey
Mentor

# Introduction

In a time when everyone is seeking to not survive but thrive as believers, *Unlocking God's Power, Favor and Blessings*, provides a fresh insight and approach to living a successful Christian life, by speaking and praying the Word of God. This will produce change in your live, your family, your business and your nation. "He that hath my word let him speak my word faithfully. Is not my word like as a fire? saith the Lord; and like a hammer that breaks the rock in pieces?" (Jeremiah 23: 28-29).

The Book's purpose is to first, rekindle within you a love for the Word of God. As you speak its truth, your passion for the principles of God's Kingdom will grow. Second, the book is an effective tool to unlock the power, favor, and blessings of God in your life. Third, the book will help you grow in your role as intercessor and joint-intercessor with Jesus Christ; who sits at the right hand of God the Father, making intercession for us.

Every Word of God spoken for your healing, your finances, your faith, and your family will prosper. Why? The Lord must act upon His Word. He says that "His Word will not return unto Him void but will accomplish that which it please." (Isaiah 55: 10)

God's power, favor and blessings, does not rest in your social standing, or your business astuteness, or your Christian service, or gender, or age. It rests in His infallible Word. The heavens and earth were formed by the spoken Word of God. Imagine the Sovereign God creating the universe by speaking and then it was.

The Bible is the inspired Word of God; it gives insight into

God's will, purpose and plan for humanity. When you read the Word, you are reading God's design for your life and the rest of humanity. The Word of God has everything that concerns your life. When you declare God's Word over your life, you are inviting God's Kingdom to come and God's will to be done in your life and on the earth. There is power in the spoken Word. The Word of God is powerful and sharper than any two-edged-sword. (Hebrews 4: 12) The Lord is quick to complete His Word (Isaiah 55: 10). Heaven and earth shall pass away but His Word will stay.

There is scriptural evidence to prove, the key to unlocking God's power, favor and blessings in our lives, is speaking the Word of God. The world was formed from the spoken Word of God. Psalm 33 verse 6 declares, "By the word of the Lord were the heavens made and all the host of them by the breath of His mouth." In Genesis chapter 1, God said *"Let there be... and there was."*

The Lord have magnified His Word above His name (Psalm 138: 2b) and according to Psalm 119 verse 89, the Word of God is settled in heaven. We can trust in the **credibility** of God's Word. God is ready to fulfill every word spoken. (Jeremiah 1: 12)

We can also trust in the **authenticity** of God's Word. "Thy word is true from the very beginning: and every one of thy righteous judgments endures forever." (Psalm 119: 160). "The grass withered, the flower fades: but the word of our God shall stand forever." (Isaiah 40: 8) From creation, the Word of God remains authentic.

We can trust in the **surety** of God's Word. "For as the rain cometh down and the snow from heaven and returns not thither but waters the earth and makes it bring forth and bud; that it may give seed to the sower and bread to the eater; So shall my Word be that goes forth out of my mouth: it shall not return unto me void, but it shall accomplish that which I please, and it shall prosper in the thing whereto I sent it." (Isaiah 55: 10-11). We can have confident assurance in the spoken Word of God. We are the mouthpiece of God to declare His word faithfully.

The Lord has given us His Word for healing and saving the nations. "He sent His word and healed them and delivered them from their destructions." (Psalm 107: 20)

He sends forth His commandment on earth: His Word runs swiftly (Psalm 147: 15). His command to us as believers is to speak His Words faithfully. "He that hath my word let him speak my word faithfully. Is not my word like as a fire? Saith the Lord; and like a hammer that breaks the rock in pieces?" (Jeremiah 23: 28-29)

The Lord has given us His Word as a powerful tool, to change our surroundings. "Is not my words like a fire.... and like a hammer that breaks the rock in pieces." (Jeremiah 23: 29) Whatever is happening around you, you have the tool to effect change; that tool is the Word of God. Jesus himself gave us the example of using the Word of God to combat the plans of the enemy. The devil tempted Jesus three times in the wilderness and three times Jesus responded, "It is written."

What better way to unlock God's power, favor and blessings in your life than speaking faithfully the Word given to us. *Unlocking God's Power, Favor and Blessings* arranges Twenty six (26) books of the Bible from the New Testament into prayer format; giving you the ability to speak and declare the Word of God faithfully over your life. Beginning each chapter, a brief introduction on the purpose and themes of the books of the bible is given.

These books of the Bible in prayer form, will allow you to

become engaged with the commands, principles and rules of God. The Scriptures will become alive in your life and the lives of those you will pray. This book will also help you to develop a deeper prayer life. It is my prayer; you will develop the habit of praying God's Word over your life. You will experience great blessings and favor because the Lord will honor His promise to be quick to perform His Word.

I pray that this book will bless you as it has blessed me and bring you into many open doors of spiritual, financial and emotional blessings.

Let the Kingdom of God come and His Will be done in and around us as we pray and declare His Word. I will hasten to perform it, says the Lord; so be quick to speak and to pray.

# Instruction for Use

Repetition is the key to learning. To profit from the prayers in this book, discipline yourself to read and read, until the truth of God's Word take root in your heart and soul; transforming your mind and your life.

Before praying the scriptural prayers, read the selected Scriptures from the Bible. Pray in faith and have a high level of expectancy; knowing that as you pray the Scriptures aloud, the truth resonating from the pages, will give heaven permission to influence your life and your surroundings.

# Gospels:

*Praying the Gospel of*

# Matthew

### Summary of the Book

The purpose of the gospels is to prove, Jesus Christ is the Messiah, the eternal King; to highlight the person of Jesus, His work and teachings; to present a correct account of the life of Christ, and to present Him as the perfect human and Savior.

Matthew was one of Jesus' twelve disciples. He wrote the gospel of Matthew to his fellow Jews, to prove, Jesus was the Messiah and to explain God's Kingdom. Matthew shows Christ power and authority over the sick, the demon controlled and the dead. The gospel of Matthew proclaims the good news: Jesus is the Christ, the King of kings and the Lord of lords, and through Him we have victory over evil and death.

As you pray this gospel, you will affirm that Jesus Christ is the King of kings and the Lord of lords. You will declare the principles and rules of His Kingdom in and around you. You will affirm the victory you have in and through His name – Jesus, the King, Messiah, Savior and Deliverer.

# Prayer # 1 – Matthew 1:1 – 6:15

Jesus, You are the Son of David and the Son of Abraham; the promised Messiah from the tribe of Judah. I worship you Lord, my God and King. You are Jesus – You came to save all people from their sins. You are Emmanuel, God who is with us. Baptize me again Oh Father with the Holy Ghost and with fire, and thoroughly purge me.

Father, for all the temptations that this world offers: the lust of the flesh, the lust of the eyes and the pride of life; help me not to surrender to them. I declare the words of Jesus, as He spoke even as He was tempted, "man shall not live by bread alone but by every word that proceeds out of the mouth of God." I declare that I will not allow any situation to cause me to tempt the Lord my God. I declare that I shall worship the Lord my God and Him only shall I serve. Lord all I need in this life is in You, and so I choose O Lord, to follow You and You alone.

Jesus, I celebrate You as Savior, Deliverer and Healer. Thank you for healing all my sicknesses and pain. You are the same yesterday, today and forever. Heal today those who are ill and in pain; heal those who are possessed by demons; heal us from all sicknesses and diseases.

Jesus, You said, blessed is the poor in spirit for the Kingdom of Heaven belongs to them. Lord I want to inherit the Kingdom of Heaven, so help me to walk in humbleness of heart. I confess my need for You Lord; without You I can do nothing.

Jesus, You also said, blessed are those who mourn for they shall be comforted. I pray for those who are mourning that You will offer comfort and encouragement. Help me Father to be gently and lowly, for only the meek shall inherit the earth. Give me a hunger and a thirsting for Your righteousness so that I am filled. Help me to be merciful. Lord I pray for a pure heart so that I will be able to see God. Help me to walk in peace as a child of God. Help me Holy Spirit to live for God, and walk in righteousness, so that I can possess the Kingdom of heaven. Holy Spirit help me also to be happy and glad when I am persecuted for righteousness sake, for great the Father says, is my reward.

I confess that I am the salt of the earth and the light of the world. I will therefore let my light shine so that everyone will see my good works and glorify my Father, who is in heaven. Father, fulfill the principles of the law in and around me. Help me Holy Spirit to practice and teach God's commandments, and walk in Christ righteousness, so that I will be able to enter the Kingdom of heaven.

Lord, remove from me anger and malice towards the brethren. Forgive me if I have spoken evil and insulting towards my brother. I commit to make peace with any who might have any grievance against me.

Holy Spirit, help me to guard my heart that I sin not against thee, through lusting. Help me Holy Spirit to cut off anything that will ensnare me, or cause me to stumble and sin. Anything that offends You, help me to rid them from my life.

Lord, I pray for husbands and wives that they will remain committed to their marriage vows and will not cause the other to sin or commit adultery.

Lord, remove from me swearing; let my communication be yes and no. Let me not retaliate against those who do evil against me. Help me Spirit of God to give to him that ask, and to him who borrows from me, let me not turn away. Help me Holy Spirit to love my enemies; to bless them that curse me, and do good unto them. Help me to pray for them, who despitefully use me and persecute me. Lord, I am unable to do this in my own strength, so I humbly ask for your help. Lord it is so easy to love those who love me and to greet only the brethren but this is not the distinguishing mark of those who are called the Sons of God. Help me to be perfect Father, help me to be perfect, as you my heavenly Father is perfect.

Lord, may my giving be marked by secrecy and not for men's recognition. Help me also when I pray and fast, to do so in secret and you my Father who sees me will reward me openly.

Father, You are aware of all my needs even before I ask of them, and so I pray as thou have instructed me: "*Our Father, which art in Heaven, Hallowed be Thy name*;" You name O Lord is Holy and there is none other like it. Your name is glorious and worthy to be praised. Father "*let Thy Kingdom come and let Thy will do done in the earth as it is in heaven.*" I pray Your Kingdom come in my home, in my family, in my community, in my church, in my government, and in my country. Let the principles of your Kingdom be established in our institutions: education, health, church, business and family. Lord I look to you as the provider and sustainer of my life; so give me today my daily bread; give me bread that is sufficient for my emotional, physical, spiritual, social and financial well-being. Forgive me Lord for all my sin, sin of omission and sin of commission, sin of disobedience and rebellion, sin of doubt and disbelief. Lord, as I look to You for forgiveness when I have wronged You; help me also to forgive others who have wronged me. Lord, lead me not into temptation but deliver me from evil. Father, deliver me from every plan of the enemy, raged against me and my family; every evil plan to hurt me and my family; every evil that is in this present world, deliver me from them, O Lord. For "*Thine is the Kingdom, and the power, and the glory, forever. Amen.*"

## Prayer # 2 – Matthew 6:19 – 9:31

Help me sovereign Lord to lay up treasures in heaven, where neither moth nor rust can corrupt nor where thieves can break through and steal. Lord, may my heart be where my treasure is and that is in heaven. Help me not to lay up treasures in this world which will fade away.

Lord, You are my Master and You alone will I serve. Forgive me for the many times I have worried myself about food or clothing or drink, when You have instructed me not to. Lord, You feed the fowls of the air and arrayed the lilies of the field, and they neither reap nor gather into barns nor toil or spin but You feed them. I am so much more valuable than these, and so I cast away worry and anxiety because worry doesn't add anything to my life. Forgive me O Lord for my little faith. I declare therefore that I will not take thought of what I shall eat or what I shall drink or wherewith shall I be clothed because you Father already knows that I am in need of these. Help me instead to seek after the Kingdom of God and His righteousness, and all I need, will be added unto me.

Forgive me Father for where I have judged, criticized or condemned others. Judge not you said that I be not judged. Let me deal with my own internal issues before I try to deal with the issues affecting others; then will I be able to help my brother.

Lord I believe that when I ask, it will be given to me and when I seek, I shall find, and when I knock, It shall be opened unto me. Lord I believe because Your Word said *"Everyone who ask receives and he that seek finds and to him that knock, it shall be opened."* Thank you Father for the good gifts you will give unto me when I ask. Help me Spirit of God to do unto others whatsoever I would have wanted them to do unto me

Keep me O God on the straight and narrow path; guide my feet from straying towards the wide and broad gate that leads to destruction. I desire life Lord; grant unto me life.

✓ Lord, let my behavior and conduct, be one that brings forth good fruit. Let others know me by my good fruit. Help me to do the will of the Father which is in heaven. Help me to build my life upon the teachings of your Word. Let me be like the wise man who built his house upon the rock, so that when the trials and temptations of this life confronts me, I will not fall but remain firm upon the foundation of your Word.

Father like the leper and the Centurion's servant, and Peter's mother-in-law, whom you healed; I pray You will heal those who may be sick in their body; stretch forth Your hand or send your Word that will effect healing in their body, mind, soul and spirit. Let their faith arise O Lord. Lord, You took our infirmities and bore our sicknesses, and it is upon that basis that I claim my healing; healing for my family and friends; healing for my community and country.

Lord I choose to follow You wherever You go. Lead me as I follow.

Lord, You are Lord over the winds and even the seas obey You. Father, rebuke the winds and the seas that are raging in and around us, and let there be a great calm. Rebuke the winds of immorality and lawlessness. Rebuke the winds of divorce and marital abuse. Rebuke the winds of poverty and lack. Rebuke the winds of sicknesses and diseases. Remove from us fear, and help us to walk in faith because there is nothing impossible with You, God our Father.

O Lord, I rejoice that You have power on earth to forgive sins. Thank you for forgiving me of my sins. Thank you that You did not come to call the righteous but sinners to repentance. Lord thank you for forgiving, and for saving me a sinner.

Father, as I rid myself of the old man, pour out Your new wine upon me and preserve me.

Lord I believe that You are able to heal me, deliver me and provide for me. Let it be unto me according to my faith. Amen!

# Prayer # 3 – Matthew 9:35 – 12:21

Lord, grant unto me a heart of compassion for the faint and those who wander as having no shepherd. Lord as it was then, so is it now; the harvest is indeed plenteous but the laborers are few. I pray Oh Father, as You have instructed, to send forth laborers into the harvest. Send me Lord as one of Your laborer to offer the message of hope, forgiveness and reconciliation to those who are lost.

Lord, I pray that the message of the Kingdom will continue to be proclaimed. Let the Spirit's power rest upon the church that we may exercise the authority to heal the sick, cast out devils, and raise the dead.

Help me as a believer to be wise as a serpent and harmless as a dove, as I carry out the work of the ministry in an evil world. Lord in the midst of persecutions cause me to endure to the end that I might be saved.

Father, as I perform the work of the ministry, remove from me fear; all fear and intimidation. I choose not to fear as You have instructed: "Fear not them which kill the body but are not able to kill the soul; but rather fear him which is able to destroy both soul and body in hell." Lord, You will not allow anything to happen to me that you do not permit, and so I choose not to fear the situations and circumstances around me. I will confess Christ before all men. Jesus may You confess me also before Your Father and Father of us all.

Lord I choose You above all and love You above all else. I am determined to take up my cross and to follow You all the way. To You I give my life. It is no longer mine. I lose myself so that I can only be found in You.

Lord, let the Holy Spirit help me never to let my conditions cause me to become offended of You.

Lord I cast all my heavy burdens and cares upon You; may I find rest in You. I choose Your yoke because Your yoke is easy and Your burden is light. Lord I choose to learn from You. You are meek and lowly in heart; may I experience rest in my soul.

In Your name Lord, I put my trust. Thank you for obtaining my victory. Amen!

# Prayer# 4 – Matthew 12:22 – 15:23

Lord, You have power to cast out devils and demons by the Spirit of God; a sign that Your Kingdom has come. I am with You Lord and not against You. Guard my heart and my lips from committing the sin of blasphemy against the Holy Ghost.

Father, Your Word says, *"a good man out of the good treasure of the heart brings forth good things; and an evil man out of the evil treasure brings forth evil things;"* May my heart be full of good treasures so that my words be justified and not be condemned.

Oh Father, give me eyes to see and ears to hear, and a heart to understand. Give my family, my community and the nations' eyes to see and ears to hear, and an understanding heart that they become converted, and receive Your healing. I pray that the heart of the unconverted would become good soil for the Word of God that they may hear and understand Your Word and bring forth fruit unto righteousness. I come against the cares of this life and the deceitfulness of riches that would choke the Word out of the heart of the new believer. May those who have accepted You as their Lord and Savior, have root in themselves, for the Word of God to strive.

Father, I await in anticipation for the day when the righteous shall shine forth as the sun in the Kingdom of the Father. Let the Kingdom of God continue to expand. Help me Spirit of God to value the Kingdom, and to put nothing else above it

Lord Jesus, like the miracle with the five loaves and two fishes, I pray that thou would blessed all that I have, and may it be multiplied back to me a hundred fold. You are the sovereign Lord, my provider. Lord, thank you for the overflow.

Lord, You are Lord over land and sea. Let me not become frightened by the raging wind that is contrary to me. Help me sovereign Lord to keep my eyes upon You, and not the circumstances around me. Remove from me lack of faith and doubt, and help me to trust in God's power over every element in this world.

Lord, forgive me where I have made the commandment of God of none effect by my traditions. Forgive me for not honoring my father and my mother as you have commanded me. Forgive me for not forgiving or loving others. Forgive me Lord of every man made traditions that have stagnated the power and glory of God in my life, and in my church. Lord, cleanse and guard my heart from evil thoughts, murder, adultery, fornication, theft, false witness, and blasphemy. These are the things that defile a man. Where I have defiled myself with these, I ask for Your cleansing and your forgiveness.

Father, grant unto me the faith of the woman of Canaan who cried unto thee, *"Have mercy on me, O Lord, thou Son of David...... Lord help me."* and you responded, *"O woman great is thy faith, be it unto thee even as thou wilt."* Lord let it be done unto me according to my faith. In Jesus' name. Amen

## ✓ Prayer # 5 – Matthew 15:29 – 18:35

Lord I worship You. You are indeed our Jehovah Rapha, the Lord that heals. I bring to You Lord, those who are lame, blind, dumb, maimed whether physically or spiritually, and I pray that You will heal them all. I place before You those lying on the hospital beds, those lying and wandering on the streets, those in homes and shelters; I pray for their healing. Lord, You are an awesome God, the God of miracles and power. You are the same God that fed the multitude with just seven loaves and a few fishes. How great thou art, my God. How great thou art. There is nothing impossible with You and I worship You. I worship You. You are indeed the Christ; the Son of the living God.

Father, I thank you for the church, and I declare that the gates of hell will never prevail against it. Lord, grant unto me the keys of the Kingdom of heaven that whatsoever I bind on earth shall be bound in heaven, and whatsoever I loose on earth shall be loosed in heaven. By faith I bind every plan that the enemy has forged against my family, my marriage, my children, my ministry, my church, my finances and my community. I loose God Spirit of adoption, grace, mercy, love, joy, peace, patience, righteousness, and justice, in the Name of Jesus Christ

Father, I choose to deny myself and to take up Your cross, and follow after You. I choose to lose my life so that I can find it in You. Lord, I let go of all my plans so that Your purpose can be fulfilled in me. I let go of the pleasures and riches of this world that is characterized by greed and selfish ambitions, so that the pleasures and riches of the Kingdom can be fulfilled in me; pleasures that are characterized by righteousness, goodness, peace, love, contentment, and joy. Lord, there is nothing in this world that I would gain in exchange for my soul.

Father, I confess that at times I have not believed as I should, and I ask for your forgiveness. I pray for the faith like the grain of a mustard seed that will enable me to command the mountains in my life and around me to be removed. Lord, may I commit to prayer and fasting so that this faith will be evident in my life.

Thank you Lord that I am an heir and a son of the Kingdom. Therefore I am free from the practices of the kingdom of this world. I am not a stranger but a son. Help me therefore to fulfill my responsibility as a citizen, not because I am under bondage but so as not to cause offense. Thank you for your provisions that will enable me to do so.

Father, help me to humble myself as a little child, and to walk before You as little children so that I enter the Kingdom of heaven.

Father, Your Word says in this world offenses must come but woe unto that man by whom the offense comes. Lord, I rid myself of any offense that will cause me not to enter into the Kingdom of heaven or any other person from entering into the Kingdom of heaven. I cut off every relationship, every habit and conduct that is an offense or causes offense. Lord, help me not to offend anyone that would cause them to stumble. Lord I pray for those who have gone astray; help me to go after them and help them to be reconciled to the faith. Lord, it is not Your will that any of these little ones perished. Save our children and bring back the back-sliders.

Father, I commit my relationships with the brethren to You, help me to deal with the offence of others against me in the right way. As You have instructed, if "a brother shall trespass against me I must go and tell him and him alone of his faults but if he refuses to listen, I must take two or three witnesses". Lord sometimes I am guilty of telling others of my brother's fault before taking it to him or her. Please forgive me. I pray that the body of Christ will follow Your principles of reconciliation and restoration. You have given us the authority to bind and loose in earth and in heaven. I pray for the power of agreement in our prayers that as we gather to pray in agreement, Your presence will be in our midst and our request shall be done of You, our Father which is in heaven.

Lord, as You have forgiven me of all my trespasses, I choose to forgive my brothers of all their trespasses. Let me not hold or carry any grudge against the brethren but to always walk in forgiveness. Right now Father if there is any unforgiveness in my heart towards another, I release it unto You and I choose to walk in forgiveness. Help me to do so when it seems difficult Lord. In Jesus' name, I pray Amen.

## Prayer # 6 – Matthew 19:1 – 22:40

Father, I thank you for the institution of marriage that You established from the beginning. Lord, this institution is coming under so many attacks, in our day and age. But you have said, "what God has joined together let no man put asunder." I pray against divorce and its causes. I pray that husbands will recognize their responsibility to cleave unto their wives and to become one with them. Marriage is a permanent institution; may those who desire to enter therein receive your instruction in obedience.

Father, Your Word says that "a rich man shall hardly enter into the kingdom of God. It is easier for a camel to go through the eye of a needle than for a rich man to enter into the Kingdom of God." The disciples were amazed and asked "who then can be saved?" With men this is impossible but with You all things are possible." And so Lord I pray for those who possess great wealth and don't see their need for You. They hide their pains, their longings and their loneliness in their possessions and acquisition of things. Lord deliver them from the deceitfulness of riches, and cause them to come into the knowledge and truth that happiness and fulfillment comes from a life surrendered to You. Save them and deliver them from the god of this age, and may they use their wealth, not to add upon the lusting of their flesh but for the greater good; the advancement of the Kingdom of God.

Father, may I walk before You and others with a servant heart. I pray for those who are leaders and ministers that they do not exercise dominion or great authority over those they lead but that they become servants of the people. Lord, even You the Son of man did not come to be ministered unto but to give your life a ransom for many.

Father, I confess that Your House is indeed a house of prayer. It is a place where the blind and the lame can be healed; where hearts and mind can be restored. Forgive me for the times I have neglected to pray and seek the healing of others. Lord Jesus, You continue to do wonderful things in our midst and so I declare Hosanna to the Son of David. Hosanna in the highest. Thank you Lord that all things, whatsoever I ask in prayer, believing; I shall receive. I cast away all doubts and I choose to walk in faith.

Help me O Lord to be worthy of entry into Your Kingdom. Let me be clothed with the right wedding garments. Cast me not away from thy presence my King. Thank you for calling me and choosing me to be a partaker of the Kingdom of God. I am grateful Father, for many others are called, but few chosen.

My Lord, my God, I commit to love You with all my heart and with all my soul and with all my mind and to love my neighbor as myself. On these two commandments hang all the law and the prophets.

# Prayer # 7 – Matthew 23: 1 – 28:20

Lord I pray against the attitude of leaders in our country and churches that place heavy burdens upon your people. I pray against those who serve in their offices for personal gains and men's approval; those who *"love the uppermost rooms at feasts and the chief seats in the synagogues and greetings in the market place"*. Lord, You alone are Master and Father; let me not give Your authority to men. Let those who have been called to lead become servants of all; may they serve with humility and not pride. Lord let everyone who exalt himself be abased and everyone who humbles himself be exalted. Father I pray against those who prevent others from entering the Kingdom of God. Woe unto them that oppresses the poor. Woe unto those who discredit the temple of God. Woe unto those who forget the weightier matters of law, judgment, mercy and faith. Woe unto those who appear clean on the outside but who are filled with dead men's bones and all uncleanness. They appear outwardly righteous unto men but within they are full of hypocrisy and iniquity. Lord, give us leaders with pure motives; leaders who love justice, mercy, righteousness and uprightness.

Lord as I await Your return, I pray that You guard my heart from becoming deceived by those who will come claiming to be Christ. Lord, help me not to become troubled by the disasters that will take place before Your return. These things must come to pass before the end comes. Help me not to become alarmed. Lord I pray for the Jews that they be delivered from the afflictions of their enemies and those who hate them; for Your name sake. Grant me wisdom Lord in how to respond in this present age where iniquity is abounding and men's heart is waxing cold. Give me a spirit of endurance to endure to the end, so I shall be saved. Let the gospel of the Kingdom be preached in the entire world for a witness unto all nations Oh God, I look forward in great anticipation for the day when the Son of man will come in the clouds of heaven with power and great glory, to gather his children from one end of the heaven to another. Even so, come Lord Jesus, come. Father no one knows the hour when Christ shall come but You. Help us therefore to be watchful and to be ready for His coming.

Lord, You have made us servants and co-laborers with Christ Jesus. Help me to be faithful over what you have given me, and may Christ upon His return find me faithfully serving.

As I serve Lord, help me to be like the five wise virgins who were prepared for the coming of the bridegroom. Help me not to become complacent but to be ready and watchful at all times. Help me to be watchful in prayer and in Your Word. Lord I want to be like the servant with the talents who were productive and gained more than what You had given unto them. When You return, may You say unto me "Well done, thou good and faithful servant." O Father I want to enter into the joy of the Lord. Give me O God, a heart for the poor; the helpless, the stranger and the imprisoned. Show me ways in how I can serve them as service to You. I pray for Your heart, Your compassion, and Your love for the least among us.

Father I thank you for Your body and Your blood; the blood of the new testament which was shed for many, for the remission of sins. I thank you for my cleansing. Lord I look forward to the day when You shall drink this fruit of the vine new with us in Your Fathers' kingdom. Lord Jesus, thank you for surrendering Your will to that of the Father and died on a cruel cross that I might be freed from the penalty of sin. Help me each day to surrender my will and declare as thou hast declared in that garden of Gethsemane, *"Not as I will but as thou wilt."*

Holy Spirit, help me to be watchful so that I enter not into temptation. The flesh is always weak so help me to walk in the Spirit, who is always willing.

Father renew within me the commission to go and teach all nations, baptizing them in the name of the Father, and of the Son, and of the Holy Ghost, and teaching them to observe all things You have taught us. Father I will go in the power and authority of Your name. In Jesus' name I pray Amen!

*Praying The Gospel of*

# Mark

## Summary of the Book

The gospel of Mark portrays Jesus as a man of action divinely capable of healing the sick, controlling nature and battling the powers of Satan. There is therefore emphasis on the message and ministry of Jesus as the servant of God. Mark shows us the humanity of Jesus, the importance of faith, and the cost of discipleship.

As you pray Mark, you will confess Jesus Christ as the Son of God having power to heal and to change circumstances. Whatever your condition as you pray believe that Jesus will deliver, heal, restore, and set free.

## Let us Pray:
# Prayer # 1 – Mark 1:1 – 4:20

Jesus Christ, I confess that thou art the Son of God. God's beloved Son in whom He is well pleased. Lord Jesus, help me to continue to proclaim the Gospel of the Kingdom and like the disciples forsake all to follow You.

Lord Jesus, You are the Holy One of God and at Your command, demons flee, the captives are freed, and the sick are healed.

Lord, through Your Holy Spirit, help me to live a life of prayer as You so often demonstrated by departing, into a solitary place to pray.

Thank you Jesus for having compassion on me as You did the leper and have cleansed me and made me clean. You are indeed the Son of God and the Son of man with power on earth to forgive sins and to deliver.

Jesus, I thank you for coming to call sinners to repentance. I confess that I am a sinner; make me over into a new vessel that will be filled with the newness of Christ.

You, O Lord, are the Lord of the Sabbath. You have power and authority to cast out demons and devils. I believe in the power of the Holy Spirit's work throughout all creation.

Father with the aid of the Holy Spirit, help me to do Your will. May I receive the Word and may it spring up and bring forth fruit in my life.

Lord, I pray for those who have heard the Word and have accepted Your Word but have allowed the enemy to take away the Word from their hearts. They have allowed persecutions and the deceitfulness of riches to choke the Word, causing it to become unfruitful. I pray that You will give them a heart that will keep and sustain your Word that they may bring forth fruit unto righteousness. I pray against the tactics and devices Satan will use to take away Your Word that was sown in their hearts. I pray against every affliction and persecution that will cause them to be offended. Lord, give them a spirit and heart of perseverance in the midst of their afflictions. Lord I pray that You will guard their hearts from the deceitfulness of riches and the lust of other things that will choke the Word sown in their hearts. I pray for hearts that are ready to receive the Word of God and will spring up into fruitfulness.

# Prayer # 2 – Mark 4:35 – 6:6

Lord, You are the Lord of the storm, wind, and the waves. At Your command they are still. Father like the disciples on that stormy sea, when the storms of life rage in my life, I am sometimes fearful but Father I declare Your words, "Peace be still" to every storm raging in and around me. Help me Lord, to find rest and peace in my storms, knowing that You will carry me safely to land.

Father, like the man with the unclean spirit in Gadarene, so are many today who are possessed by legions and creating havoc in our communities. Father in the name of Jesus and the power of the Holy Spirit, I pray for their deliverance. I command every demon to come out of them in the name of Jesus Christ. I command them to come out of our men and young men; our women and young women who are giving themselves to prostitution and all kinds of immorality. In Jesus' name, I pray.

Lord give me the faith of the woman with the issue of blood to press into You until I have touched Your garment; making me whole. O Lord, increase my faith to believe. Guard my heart from becoming hardened at the works of Your hand and the demonstration of Your power.

Lord Jesus, I am not offended by You. I believe that You are the Son of God with power and wisdom to do mighty works. To You Lord I ascribe honor, power and majesty. Do a mighty work in my life and in the lives of others. Remove from me any form of unbelief.

## Prayer # 3 – Mark 6:7 – 8:38

Lord I pray for those whom You have called (preachers, teachers, evangelists, prophets); may they go forth with power over unclean spirits and preach to men their repentance. Let the demonstration of Christ's power be evident in their ministry, to cast out demons and heal the sick through the anointing oil.

Father in the midst of such chaos and busyness in this world, may we find time to come aside and rest in You.

Lord, You are indeed a Miracle worker. I ask You to provide for those who are in need and make whole those who are sick in body. Lord, forgive me for the times when I honored You only with my lips but my heart was far from You. Lord, forgive me for the times I have held unto the traditions of men instead of obeying the commandments of God. Forgive me for when I have made the Word of God of none effect through my traditions. Forgive me O Lord.

Lord, guard my heart from all things that would defile me and make me unclean: evil thoughts, adultery, fornication, murder, theft, covetousness, wickedness, deceit, lasciviousness, evil-eye, blasphemy, pride and all foolishness. All these evil things come from within and defile us. Grant unto me a clean heart; a pure heart, O Lord.

Lord, You are the Lord who has done all things well. You make both the deaf to hear and the dumb to speak. You fed the four thousand with just seven loaves and two fishes. You healed the blind man. You are a great God.

Lord I confess like Peter that You are the Christ. I choose to follow You. I deny the selfish things of this world and I choose to take up my cross and follow You. I am not ashamed of Your words. I believe that You are the Christ.

# Prayer # 4 – Mark 9:19 – 11:9

Father, You said if we believe, all things are possible to him that believes. Lord I believe. I believe in Your power to heal me, to deliver me, to deliver my family, and to deliver this nation. I believe O Lord in Your name. Help me to live in prayer and fasting so that the power of God may be at work in my life.

Lord I cut off everything from my life that will cause me to stumble and not enter into the Kingdom of God. Let the salt of my life be good, and may I walk in peace with others.

Lord, I pray for marriages. I pray against the hardness of the hearts of husbands and wives, who want to forsake their covenant. I pray instead that they will cleave unto each other; that they will become one. I pray against all internal and external forces that are affecting married persons, and I declare Your Word against the enemy that what therefore God has joined together, let no man put asunder.

Lord I pray for the children that others will not hinder them from coming to you, for of such is the Kingdom of God. Give me Lord child-like faith and trust that I may enter the Kingdom of God. Lay Your hands upon our children and blessed them.

Lord, with You all things are possible and so I pray for those who trust in riches to the effect that it will affect their entry into the Kingdom of God. Lord, deliver them from the deceitfulness of riches and save them. Let their trust be in You and You only.

Lord I pray for those whom You have entrusted with the ability to lead that they will have a servant heart, and will not exercise lord-ship over those they lead. For whomsoever will be great among us shall be our minister, and whosoever will be chief, shall be servant of all. Lord, You gave the example of a true servant. You came not to be ministered unto but to minister and give Your life a ransom for us all.

Lord, may I have the faith, persistence and desperation that blind Bartimaeus had that thou others around me want to hold me back, I will cry out, *"O thou Son of David have mercy on me!"* Help me to cast away my garments and come to You.

Blessed are You O Lord who cometh in the name of the Lord. We cry Hosanna! Hosanna! Hosanna in the Highest! Amen

## Prayer # 5 – Mark 11:15 – 16:18

Lord, forgive me for when I have engaged in so many activities in Your house rather than the activity of prayer. Lord I confess that Your house, the physical place of worship, and my body, the temple of the Holy Spirit, shall be a house of prayer. Lord, increase my faith. Remove every doubt in my heart and help me to believe that those things which I shall say shall come to pass. Lord even now as I pray, I believe that I shall receive all that I ask for and shall have them.

Lord if there is any unforgiveness in my heart, I give it to You. I choose to forgive anyone who may have wronged me in anyway. I release them Father because I need your forgiveness. You said If I will not forgive, You will not forgive me my trespasses.

I confess that the Lord our God, is one Lord. There is none other but you Lord. I choose to love You Lord with all my heart, with all my soul, with my entire mind, and with all my strength. I choose also to love my neighbor as myself. This is more than all whole burnt offerings and sacrifices.

Lord, help me to give not only out of my abundance but out of my want.

Lord, prepare me for the forthcoming woes to be upon the earth. Help me to endure to the end that I might be saved.

Lord, I look with great anticipation when You shall come in the clouds with great power and glory, and You shall send forth Your angels to gather Your elect from the four winds, from the uttermost part of the earth to the uttermost part of the heaven. Heaven and earth shall pass away but Your words shall not pass away. Help me Spirit of the Living God to be watchful and not to allow the coming of Christ to find me sleeping.

Father, I thank you for the body of Christ and for the blood of the new testament which was shed for many. Help me Father to watch and pray, lest I enter into temptation.

O Father, I thank you for Jesus' death and burial but more so for His resurrection. Lord, refresh our mandate and commission to go into the world and preach the Gospel to every creature. Father as we believe, cause Your signs to follow us. In Your name, cause us to cast out devils. Make us speak with new tongues. Cause us to lay hands on the sick and they shall recover, in Jesus' name, Amen!

*Praying the Gospel of*

# Luke

## Summary of the Book

The gospel of Luke portrays Jesus' divinity and His humanity. Jesus the Son of God is the Son of Man. As you pray Luke, you will pray God's sovereignty over humanity and over your own life.

## Let us pray:
# Prayer # 1 – Luke 1:46 – 4:28

Lord, who is like unto You? For with You nothing shall be impossible. Father like Mary, my soul doth magnify You and my spirit rejoices in You my Savior. For You have done great things and holy is Your name. Your mercy O Lord is on them who fear You, from generation to generation. Lord, You have shown strength with Your arm and have scattered the proud in the imagination of their hearts. You have put down the mighty from their seats and exalted them of low degree. You have filled the hungry with good things and the rich You have sent away empty. Lord, continue to help Your servant Israel in remembrance of Your mercy.

Blessed are thou O Lord, the God of Israel. Thank you for having risen up a horn of salvation for us. Thank you that from of old, thou hast spoken by the mouth of Your holy prophets that we should be saved from our enemies and from the hand of all who hates us; to serve you without fear, in holiness and righteousness, all the days of our lives.

Father like John, may we prepare the way of salvation for others. Help us to give the knowledge of salvation to all people through the remission of sin, and the tender mercy of God our Father. O Lord, continue to give light to those who sit in darkness and in the shadow of death, and guide our feet into the way of peace.

Father, I thank you for the good-tidings of great joy; Jesus who is Savior and Christ the Lord. I thank you, that You have allowed me to see the salvation of God. Help me to bring forth fruit worthy of repentance. Baptize me again O Lord with the Holy Ghost and with fire.

Father the enemy continues to come at me on all fronts but

as You withstood him in the wilderness, I withstand him also, and declare that man shall not live by bread alone but by every Word of God. I declare that I shall worship the Lord my God and Him only shall I serve. I will not allow the enemy to cause me to tempt You, Lord my God.

I thank you Father for the Gospel. I thank you for coming and healing my broken heart. I thank you for delivering me from captivity and recovering my sight. I thank you for liberating me. I thank you Father for the acceptable year of the Lord; the year of God's favor. Father may the same Spirit and anointing that rest on Jesus, now rest on me. I will continue in the mission to preach the Gospel to the poor, to heal the broken hearted, to preach deliverance to those who are still held in captivity, and to set at liberty them that are bruised.

Lord, I want to be like the widow of Sarepta to whom Elijah was sent during the famine, and like Naaman the Syrian, who was cleansed by Elisha. They were obedient to Your command. Whatever You are doing don't do it without me. Give me a willing and a ready spirit.

# Prayer # 2 – Luke 4:38 – 6:26

Lord Jesus, You are the Holy One of God with power and authority to destroy demons and devils. Lord in Your name, I command every unclean spirit that has been tormenting Your people, to come out of them, in Jesus' name! Lord I rebuke sicknesses and diseases. Lord let Your anointing flow through the palm of my hands so that when I lay my hands on the sick, they shall be healed.

Lord, though things may look dim around me, nevertheless at thy Word, I will launch out into the deep. At Your Word Lord, I will do and I will be.

Lord thank you that it is Your will that I might be clean.

Lord, as you withdrew from the crowd so many times to pray. Help me Father to withdraw from the busyness of this life to meet with You in prayer.

Oh Father, let the power of the Lord be present in our church, to effect healing in the lives of Your people. Jesus, Son of man, You have power upon earth to forgive sins, and I glorify You for that.

Father, like Levi, help me not to hesitate, to leave all and follow You. I thank you Lord for coming, not to call the righteous but sinners to repentance.

Lord, give me new wine skin that my new wine will be preserved. Lord I desire newness; bring me into newness of the letter.

Lord, remove from me any trace of attitude of the scribes and Pharisees, who were blinded to the truth and were more misguided about the Law.

Lord, let healing virtue flow from You to all those who are sick of all manner of sicknesses and diseases; may all of them be healed in Your name.

Father, let the poor realize that they are blessed because to them belong the Kingdom of God. Let those who hunger now know that they are blessed because they shall be filled. Let those who weep now, rejoice for they shall laugh again. Let those who are hated and ostracized know that they are blessed because their reward is great in heaven. I declare that I am blessed no matter what my circumstance.

Father I declare woe unto the rich for they have received their consolation. Woe unto those who are full for they shall be hungry. Woe unto them which laugh now, for they shall mourn and weep. Woe unto all men that speak evil of us.

Lord, let me be a recipient of your blessings and not your wrath.

# Prayer # 3 – Luke 6:27 – 7:10

Sweet Holy Spirit, help me to love my enemies, and to do good to them which hate me. Help me to bless them that curse me, and to pray for them who despitefully use me. Help me to give to those who ask me. As I would that men should do unto me, help me to do even so to them. Oh Father, as You have instructed me, I confess that I will love my enemies. I will do good to them and lend hoping for nothing again. Lord, I thank you that my reward will be great in heaven, and I shall be considered a child of the highest. You, O Lord, are kind unto the unthankful and to the evil. Holy Spirit, help me to be merciful even as the Father is merciful.

Father, forgive me for judging and condemning others. I do not want to be judged, so I will not judge. I do not want to be condemned, so I will not condemn others. I want to be forgiven and so I will forgive others.

Lord, give me a kind and giving heart. I pray that when I give I shall receive. *"It shall be given unto me good measure, pressed down and shaken together and running over, shall all men given into my bosom."* Lord the same measure I give will be the same measure it is going to be measured unto me again. I choose therefore to be kind and forgiving of others. Help me not to judge. Help me to deal with the beam in my own eye so that I will be able to see clearly to pull out the mote that is in my brother's eye.

Lord I want to be like a good tree that brings forth good fruit; for a good man out of the good treasure of his heart brings forth that which is good. Lord I want to produce that which is good. Give me a good heart and not an evil heart because an evil man out of the evil treasure of his heart brings forth that which is evil.

Lord my foundation shall be in You, so when the floods of life arise and the streams of life beat vehemently; I will not be shaken but my life will be found deep in You. Lord, You are my Lord and I will do what You say.

Father grant unto me, the attitude of the Centurion, who thought himself unworthy of Your presence even though others thought he was worthy. Lord help me never to think that I am worthy or deserving of something because of who others think I am or of what I think of my position. Lord I am nothing, and I am unworthy of Your presence, Your grace is what I seek.

## Prayer # 4 – Luke 8:4 – 10:42

Lord I pray for those who hear the Word that they will keep it and bring forth fruit with patience. Lord I pray against the tactics of the enemy, to try and steal the Word out of the hearts of those who hear it, that they should not believe and be saved. I pray that the Word will fall on good soil and take root that when temptation comes, they will not fall away. Lord, I pray against the situations that will choke the Word; the cares and pleasures of this life; preventing the hearers from bringing fruit to perfection. Make the hearts of people, good soil for the Word of God to be planted, and bring forth fruit that will remain. Help us O Lord to take heed to what we hear and to do it.

Lord God, You are Lord of the wind and the water. You command the wind and the wave and they obey You. In Your name Jesus, I speak to every wind and wave in my life and my family, and I command them to cease. I thank you Father for the calmness, in Jesus' name.

Father, I will publish the great things that Jesus has done. You are our deliverer and our healer. Lord, like the Gadarene Demoniac, deliver all who are possessed and tormented by demons, in Jesus' name. Like the woman with the issue of blood, let virtue flow from thee and heal all who are sick.

Lord, thank you for the power and the authority that You have given to us, over all devils and diseases. Like the disciples, help us to continue with boldness in preaching the Kingdom of God, and healing the sick.

Lord, I choose to come after You. Help me to deny myself and to take up my cross daily and follow You. Lord I am willing to lose my life for Your sake. I will not be ashamed of You nor Your Word. Help those who are outside of Your will to know that it is no advantage to them to gain the whole world and lose their soul.

Lord, I thank you that You did not come to destroy men lives but to save them. Help me to have this attitude in my dealings with those who would oppose our teachings and our faith.

Lord, as You have instructed; I pray for the harvest that You will send forth workers. Here I am Lord, send me.

Lord, I pray that my church and ministry will be infused with power from high; power to tread on serpents and scorpions; power over all the power of the enemy. I declare that nothing shall by any means harm me. Lord, help me to rejoice that my name is written in heaven and not in my ability to use Your power.

Father, I join in praise as Jesus did, and in thanksgiving. You are Lord of heaven and earth. You have hid things from the wise and prudent, and have revealed them unto babes. Thank you for the privileges of seeing and hearing things which the prophets and kings of old had desired to see and had not seen, and to hear and had not heard.

Lord, I commit today to love You, with all my heart and with all my soul, and with all my strength, and with all my mind; and my neighbor, will I love like myself. Help me heavenly Father to be merciful unto all people.

Lord I must confess that sometimes like Martha, I become encumbered about with much serving, neglecting that which is needful, and that is to sit at your feet, and learn from you, as Mary did.

In Jesus' name I pray, Amen.

# Prayer # 5 – Luke 11:1 – 14:35

Lord, as You taught the disciples to pray, I acknowledge that You are Our Father and that Your name is Holy. Father, I pray that Your Kingdom will come in and among us, and that Your will be done on earth, as it is in heaven. Father, I look to You for my daily sustenance; so give unto me my daily bread. Forgive me of all my sins. I commit to forgive everyone who has wronged me. Father, lead me not into temptation but deliver me from every evil. Thank you Father.

Lord, give me a spirit of importunity. Help me Holy Spirit to ask, seek and knock until doors are opened unto me. Lord you said "ask and it shall be given unto me; seek and I shall find; knock and it shall be opened unto me; for everyone that ask receives and he that seeks, finds and to him that knock, it shall be opened."I thank you Lord for hearing me and answering my petitions, and requests. Thank you that You are a Father that will give unto me whatsoever I ask. Grant unto me O Lord the Holy Spirit; may my life be filled with His power and glory.

Lord remove from me an evil eye and give unto me an eye that is single, so that my whole body is also full of light. I choose to walk and live in the light and not in darkness.

Lord, I will not fear what men can do unto me because they can only kill the body, but I choose to fear You, who is able to kill and cast into hell, both body and soul. I will confess You before men. Guard my lips from blaspheming against the Holy Ghost. Guard my heart from covetousness, for a man's life does not consist in the abundance of the things he possesses.

Lord, help me not to become or behave like a fool, who lay up treasures for himself and is not rich toward God. Help me Spirit of the Living God not to take thought for my life, what I shall eat or what I shall wear. Life, Your word says, is more than meat, and the body more than raiment. Father I acknowledge that I am more important than the fowls whom you feed so I will not worry because worrying cannot add any measure to my stature. Lord, forgive me for having little faith. Today, I choose to believe that You who clothe the grass, which is today in the field and tomorrow is cast into the oven, will likewise clothe me, who is of greater value. Lord, You know of the things that I need and I believe that You will provide for me. I choose therefore to seek the Kingdom of God and when I do all these things will be added unto me; all that I need for the body and for life. Father it is Your good pleasure to give unto us the Kingdom and for that I am thankful. My treasure shall be laid up in heaven where no thief can approach or moth corrupt.

Lord, let me be among those servants whom You will find watching when You come. Help me Holy Spirit to be always watching whether Christ shall come in the first, second or third watch; may he find me watching. Help me to be a faithful and wise steward over Your household and when You return, may You find me so doing.

Father in the name of Jesus Christ, I command everyone to be loosed from their infirmities. Lord Jesus, lay your hands on the sick and cause an immediate recovery so that Your name be glorified

Lord, help me to humble myself for whosoever exalts himself shall be abased and he that humbles himself shall be exalted.

I choose Lord to take up my cross and come after You. I have counted the cost and I have decided to follow you.

# Prayer # 6 – Luke 17:1 – 24:1

Father, I pray for those who are lost like the prodigal son. Let them come to themselves and return to You, who will welcome them with arms of love, forgiveness and compassion. Lord I commit all backsliders into Your hand, and I pray for their return to the Kingdom.

Lord, help me to be faithful, even in the least that has been given to me.

Holy Spirit, help me not to become an offence to anyone. Lord I choose to forgive my brother who trespasses against me, and as instructed in Your Word, should he trespass against me seven times in a day, and seven times in a day ask for my forgiveness, I will forgive him. Help me Holy Spirit to be obedient to the Word. O Lord, as the disciples asked of You, I also ask of You, to increase my faith. Lord, help me to do that which is my duty to do as a servant.

Lord, I confess that the Kingdom of God is within me. Let it be manifested in every area of my life.

Lord, I believe that You are coming back for Your church. Help me to be watchful and ready, and not to be like the people in the days of Noah and Lot. Lord, I willingly give You my life, for whosoever shall lose his life shall preserve it but whosoever shall seek to save his life shall lose it.

Help me Holy Spirit to always pray and not faint. Help me to persevere and be persistent in prayer. I pray when you return, may You find faith in me.

Lord, help me to walk before You in humility. Forgive me if I have ever acted righteously, yet despising others. Heavenly Father, like the Publican, I ask that You be merciful unto me a sinner. I am in need of Your grace and Your mercy. Lord, help me never to forget that.

Lord, I place our children before You, may You bless them, and keep Your hand upon them. Let no one offend or hurt them. Give us child like faith and trust in You Lord.

Lord, help me not to hold unto any earthly possession to the detriment of my salvation. Help me to seek after the treasures in heaven and follow after You. Lord I pray for those who have great riches that they will be saved. I pray that they will use their riches for the advancement of Your Kingdom here on earth.

Lord, for those who have left all to follow You, I pray that they will receive manifold more in this present time , and in the world to come, life everlasting.

O thou Son of David, have mercy upon me and let my faith save me. Let Your name O Lord, be glorified among the people.

Son of man, You came to seek and to save those who were lost. Lord, let salvation come to my house. Save my unsaved relatives.

Lord, I thank you that You have chosen me to be a servant in Your Kingdom. I thank you for the gifts and abilities that You have given me, to serve in Your Kingdom. Holy Spirit, help me to be faithful in what the Lord has given me. Help me to occupy faithfully until He returns. Lord reign over my life. I acknowledge You as my King.

Lord, forgive me for neglecting prayer in Your house. Your house is indeed a house of prayer. Help me Holy Spirit to be earnest in offering all kinds of prayer in Your house, above every program and activity. Let a life of prayer, be a distinguishing mark of all believer.

The stone which the builders rejected has indeed become the cornerstone, and whosoever shall fall upon it shall be broken, and whosoever it shall fall upon, shall be grounded into powder.

Father, help me to give out of my want and not out of my abundance. Like the widow's offering, let my offering be all that I have.

Lord, guard my heart from deception. As I await Your return, let me not be deceived by those who will come proclaiming that they are the Christ. Lord in the day of my persecution, I thank you, for giving me wisdom which all my adversaries will not be able to gainsay or resist. In my patience help me to possess my soul.

O Lord, heaven and earth shall pass away but not Your Word. Your Word shall not pass away. Thank you for the instructions You have given me in Your Word concerning Your return. Help me to take heed, not to let that day come upon me unawares. Help me Jesus not to become encumbered with the cares of this life but to be watchful, and to pray always that I be counted worthy to escape all these things that shall come to pass, and to stand before the Son of man.

Lord Jesus, I thank you for the broken bread which represents Your body, which was given for me. I thank you for the new testament in Your blood, which was shed for me.

Lord, grant unto me a servant attitude. Let me be among my brethren, as one who serves. Thank you Lord for appointing unto me a Kingdom, as the Father has appointed unto You. I declare that I am a child of the Kingdom of God, and the Kingdom is within me. Father, I look forward to the day when I shall eat and drink at Your table, in Your Kingdom.

Lord Jesus, I thank you that You are my High Priest, sitting at the right hand of the Father making intercession for me. I ask that You pray for me that my faith fail not in this world.

Lord I pray that I will not enter into temptation.

Jesus, I thank you for dying on the cross; bearing my sins and the sins of the world. Thank you for this expression of love.

I will forever be grateful to You and my life, I surrender to You.

You are indeed the resurrected Lord. Open my understanding that I may understand the scriptures. Help me to be a true witness of Your life, death, burial and resurrection; preaching the repentance and remission of sins in Your name, to all nations. In Jesus' name Amen!

*Praying the Book of*

# John

### Summary of the Book

The purpose of the gospel of John, is to prove Jesus is the Son of God and all who believe in Him, will have everlasting life. The author of John gives the reader a personal and powerful look at Jesus Christ, the eternal Son of God. In the book you capture the birth and preparation of Jesus, His ministry, His death, and resurrection

As you pray the book of John, you are confirming the Sonship of Jesus Christ and your confession of faith in His person, His ministry, His death, and His resurrection.

## Let us Pray:
# Prayer # 1 – John 1:1 – 5:18

Jesus Christ, Son of God, You are the Living Word. From the beginning, You were with God. Through You, all things were made and without You, was nothing made, that was made. In You I have found life; the life which was the light of men. Lord You came unto Your own but Your own received You not, but I thank you that as many as received You, You have given them power to become the Sons of God; to those who believe on Your name. I believe on Your name Jesus, and I am therefore a son of God. I am born not of the flesh or of the will of man but of the will of God.

I thank you Jesus for coming and dwelling among us. Thank you for revealing Your glory which was full of grace and truth and of Your fullness I have received, grace for grace. I thank you for declaring the Father to me. Lord, John bore record that You are the Son of God and his witness, do I believe. Jesus, You are a miracle working God. Continue to manifest Your glory and Your power.

I declare that I am born of the water and of the Spirit, and as a result, I have access to the Kingdom of God. Father, You loved me so much that You sent Your only begotten Son to earth that once I believe in Him I should not perish but have everlasting life. Father I believe in Your Son Jesus Christ and therefore have eternal life. Father, You sent not Your Son into the world to condemn the world but that the world through Him might be saved. Thank you Father. I am not condemned because I believe in Jesus.

Jesus, I thank you for giving me the living water that shall be in me a well of water springing up into everlasting life. Like the woman of Samaria, I ask of thee Lord to give me living water so I will never thirst again.

Holy Spirit, help me to become a true worshipper, who will worship the Father in Spirit and in truth. The Father seeks such to worship Him. "God is a Spirit and they that worship Him must worship Him in Spirit, and in truth." O Lord, let true worship flow within our churches and congregations. Lord, like the Samaritan woman, help me to spread the good news to my neighbors of what You have done in my life.

Lord Jesus, Your meat was to do the will of God and to finish His work. Let this be my meat; may I seek at all times to do the will of the Father, and to complete His work here on earth. The fields are white and ready to harvest. Lord let the reapers and sowers arise to do Your will and finish Your work so that both may rejoice.

Lord, You are able to heal and deliver, and so as You healed the official's son and the man at the Bethesda pool, heal those who are riddled with sicknesses and diseases in our world. I pray for a sudden and immediate healing in their lives in Your name, I pray. Amen.

# Prayer # 2 – John 5:24 – 8:32

Lord Jesus I honor You and I believe that the Father has shown You all things, and have committed judgment unto You the Son that all men should honor You. Jesus I thank you that they who hear Your Word and believe on the Father have everlasting life, and shall not come into condemnation but are passed from death to life. Jesus, I believe and I therefore have everlasting life. I am no longer condemned but have passed from death into life. I thank you Jesus.

Lord Jesus, the Father has indeed given You authority to execute judgment. Execute judgment in our world and against those who continue to walk contrary to Your word. Thank you for coming and doing the will of the Father. The works that You did bore witness that the Father had sent You that we might be saved.

Lord I seek only the honor that comes from God and not of man. I believe in Your Word.

Lord, You are the Lord of the impossible. Multiply my little and make it much, as You multiplied the five loaves and two fishes, to feed the multitude. Lord I give You what I have, and ask that You multiply it so that Your name be glorified.

Lord Jesus, You are the Lord of the sea. Walk upon the raging seas of my life. Remove from me fear. You are, I Am, and so I will not be afraid.

Lord, I seek after You not for bread but that I may know You. Help me Holy Spirit to labor not for meat that perishes but for that meat which endures unto everlasting life. Give me O Lord this meat. Lord, the work of God is to believe on You, whom He had sent. I believe Father.

Jesus, You are the bread which hath come down from heaven and gives life unto the world. You are my Bread of Life; in

You, I have found life. Because I come unto You Lord, I declare that I shall never be hungry, neither shall I ever thirst.

Lord Jesus, as the Father hath sent You, and You live by the Father, I therefore live by You because I have eaten of Thee, the Bread of Life.

Lord, You have the words of eternal life and I will turn to no one but You, whose words are spirit and life. Lord, let Your Spirit quickens me because the flesh profits nothing. Like Simon Peter, I believe, and I am sure that Thou art the Christ, the Son of the Living God.

Lord, help me not to judge according to appearance but to judge righteous judgments.

Lord, I thirst for Your righteousness, give me thereof to drink. As I believe on You, cause out of my belly to flow rivers of living water. Glorified Lord, fill me with Your Holy Spirit.

Jesus, You are the true Light; the Light of the world. They that follow You "shall not walk in darkness but shall have the Light of life." I confess that I am in the Light and will not walk in darkness. Thank you Lord for giving me the truth that has set me free. I will continue in Your Word. In Jesus' name, I pray. Amen

# Prayer # 3 – John 10:1 – 14:27

Lord, You are the Good Shepherd, who gives Your life for the sheep. I want to be in Your sheepfold. You alone will I follow, and not the voice of strangers. I thank you Lord that You came that I might have life, and have it more abundantly. Protect me and shield me from the thief, who comes to steal, to kill, and to destroy the sheep. I thank you Jesus for laying down Your life for the sheep. Thank you Lord that as Your sheep, no man can pluck me out of Your hand.

"Lord I believe, You are the resurrection and the life, and he that believeth in You, though he was dead, yet shall he live and whosoever liveth and believeth in You shall never die." I believe this Lord; show me the glory of God. Call forth every dead situation in my life and loose me Jesus, and let me go.

I choose to serve and follow You Lord Jesus. Let the Father bestow upon me His honor. I seek after Your eternal life. Glorify thy name in me Father, as You glorified Your name in Your Son Jesus. Draw me unto you O Lord. I believe in the light.

Lord I believe on You and therefore I confess You as my Lord and Savior. I'd rather the praise of God than the praise of men.

Lord Jesus, I thank you for demonstrating to me the example of true humility and servant hood, through the washing of the disciples' feet. Give me a heart of humility and servant hood.

Holy Spirit, help me to love the brethren as Christ loves me. For by this men shall know that I am Christ's disciple, if I love the brethren.

I thank you Jesus that You have gone to prepare a place for me. In the Father's house, You said, are many mansions, and You have gone to prepare a place for me, so that where You are, there I might be also. Jesus, You are the way, the truth, and the life, and no man cometh unto the Father but by You.

I believe on You Jesus and I believe that the Father is in You, and You are in the Father. I also believe You, for the works that You do. Thank you Lord that if I ask anything in Your name, You will do it that the Father may be glorified in the Son.

Lord, I love You and will therefore keep Your command-ments. Thank you for giving me another Comforter, the Holy Spirit, who will abide with me forever. He is indeed the Spirit of Truth whom the world cannot receive because it sees Him not, neither knows Him. But Lord I know Him, for He dwells within me, and is in me. I thank you Jesus for not leaving me comfortless.

Lord Jesus because You live, I live also. You are in the Father and You are in me, and I am in You. I keep Your command-ments because I love you Lord. Manifest Yourself in me and make your abode with me. Holy Spirit, I thank you for teach-ing me all things and for bringing all things to my remem-brance. I thank you for the peace that you give Lord, not as the world gives. I will therefore not be troubled neither will I be afraid because I have Your peace.

# Prayer # 4 – John 15:1 – 20:31

Lord Jesus, You are the true vine, and the Father is the husbandman. Purge me O Lord that I may bring forth more fruit. I choose to abide in You because I cannot bear fruit of myself, except I abide in You. Lord I confess that You are the vine and I am a branch; once I abide in You I will bring forth much fruit. I want to be fruitful Lord, and so I will abide and remain in You. Lord because I abide in You, and Your words abide in me, I believe that whatever I ask of Thee, it will be done unto me because I abide in You and in Your words. I want the Father to be glorified in me, by the fruits I bear. Thank you for loving me as the Father has loved You. Help me to continue in Your love. Help me Holy Spirit to keep the commandments so that I may abide in Christ's love.

Lord, let Your joy remain in me and may my joy be full. I will love the brethren as thou hast loved me. I thank you Jesus for laying down Your life for me. Thank you for calling me friend. Thank you for choosing me and ordaining me to go forth and bring forth fruit, and that my fruit should remain, and whatsoever I shall ask of the Father in Your name, You may give it to me.

I am not of this world Lord because You have chosen me out of the world. I will not become disheartened or offended therefore if the world hates me because they also hated You when You were in world.

I thank you Jesus for sending us the Comforter, the Holy Spirit who has been reproving the world of sin and righteousness, and of judgment. He has been guiding me into all truth and has been glorifying You. Lord I ask of Thee that my joy might be full.

I thank you Jesus for overcoming the world and because

You have overcome the world, so can I.

Father I thank you that indeed You have glorified Jesus Christ, Your Son, and He has also glorified Thee. You have given Him power over all flesh that He should give eternal life to as many as Thou hast given Him. Lord I thank you for allowing me to come to know the only true God and Jesus Christ, whom thou hath sent. I thank you Jesus for glorifying the Father on the earth and for finishing the work which He gave You. I thank you for manifesting the name of the Father unto us. Thank you for giving to me the words which the Father gave You. I receive them gladly and believe that the Father did indeed send You.

Jesus, continue to pray for me, for I am Yours and all that is Yours is the Father's. I want You to be glorified in me. As you asked of the Father, I also ask that the Father will keep me through His own name, and help me to be one as You and the Father are one. O Lord let Your joy be fulfilled in me. Keep me from the evil that is in the world. Sanctify me O Lord through thy Word because thy Word is truth.

Lord, help me to be one in You, as the Father is in You and You are in the Father. Thank you Jesus, for giving me Your glory that we may be one.

Lord, Your Kingdom is not of this world. You are indeed my King. For this very cause were You born and came into the world that You should bear witness unto the truth.

Thank you Jesus, that it is finished. My redemption and work of salvation is finished. My healing and deliverance is finished. My restoration and victory is finished.

The resurrected Lord, I believe that You are the Christ, the Son of God and through my belief I have obtained eternal life. I thank you Jesus. I am forever grateful for the cross and the work on Cavalry's hill. Thank you for dying for my sins and for redeeming my soul from destruction and reconciling me to the Father's love. In Jesus' name Amen!

*Praying the*

# Acts of the Apostles

## Summary of the Book:

The Acts of the Apostles explains the origin, growth and expansion of the early church, starting from the ascension of Jesus. When reading the book of Acts you get the sense of unity, the spirit of community, love, companionship, and service among the members of the early church. The book also highlights the various persecutions the early followers of Christ experienced and the joy that they displayed in the midst of the persecutions. We also experience the work and power of the Holy Spirit in the life of the early church, in spreading the Gospel and the commitment to prayer by the early believers.

As you pray the Acts of the Apostles you will be captivated by the spirit and bond of unity, love, community, fellowship and the ministry of evangelism that was apparent in the early church and will develop the zeal and passion to share the good news with others

## Let us Pray:
# Prayer # 1 – Acts 2:1 – 4:13

Lord Jesus, You have ascended on high and now sit at the right Hand of the Father making intercession for me. I thank you for reconciling me to the Father and for redeeming my soul from destruction. I thank you for giving me the Holy Spirit, who has been guiding me, into all truth. God had made You, who was crucified, both Lord and Christ.

Heavenly Father, I asked that You fill me again with the Holy Spirit. Like the day of Pentecost, let Your Holy Spirit come upon me and come in me, like a mighty rushing wind. Let tongues of fire rest upon me. Lord, I pray for the unity of the Church. Help me to be in one accord with the brethren, so that I can experience a supernatural outpouring of the Holy Spirit's power.

Lord, pour out Your Spirit upon all flesh. Let Your sons and daughters prophesy. Your young men see visions and old men dream dreams. Lord the promise of the Holy Spirit is unto us and unto our children, and to all who are afar off, as many as You will call. Let wonders be seen in the heavens above and signs in the earth below; blood and fire, and vapor of smoke, before that great and notable day of the Lord.

Lord, let everyone who calls upon Your name be saved. Help me as a believer to continue steadfast in the Word of God, in fellowship, in the breaking of bread, and in prayers. Lord, I ask that You add to the church daily. I recommit myself to the work of the Holy Spirit, the fellowship of the believers, in love and community. Lord may I serve You with gladness of heart. Let my praise be continually of You. I also ask Lord, for favor with all people, so Your church can grow.

Lord, we have the message of hope that Jesus is the answer

and the Holy Spirit so we can give hope to others in need of hope; in our home, the church and the world. Lord, help us as a church, to give unto the people that which is necessary for life and growth. Help us to operate in the demonstration of the Spirit's power, to set the captives free, to heal the lame, and to lose the oppressed.

Lord, I pray for all unsaved persons that upon hearing the good news, they will repent and be converted. I pray their sins will be blotted out, and they will experience the times of refreshing that comes from Your presence. Bless them O Lord and turn every one of them from their iniquities.

Lord, indeed the stone which was set at naught has become the head of the corner, and there is Salvation in none other than Jesus Christ. There is no name under heaven given among men whereby they must be saved but the name of Jesus. Amen!

# Prayer # 2 – Acts 4:23 – 5:42

Lord grant unto Your servants' boldness to speak Your Word, and let there be increase signs and wonders through Your holy name. Lord I need another touch from the Holy Ghost. Without His power I can do nothing. Empower me again that I may speak the Word of God boldly in every setting.

Lord, give the church one heart and one soul. Let us share all things in common with those of the household of faith. Lord I may not have great possessions but whatever I have, let me share with those who may not have. Lord let a great measure of Your grace come upon me.

Father let the reverential fear of God come in our churches that we may walk before You in truth and awe.

Lord, I pray for a supernatural outpouring of Your Spirit's power upon me, and like Peter, may my very shadow heal the sick and the oppressed. Let signs and wonders be wrought among the people that many will be added to the church.

Father, I thank you that no one can overthrow the church. The very gates of hell, Your Word says, cannot prevail against it. Lord, from the days of the early church, men tried to silence the Apostles but to no avail. We thank you that the Gospel, the goods news of Christ, continues to be preached, and men are still being saved from their sins. Lord, help me not to become weary in spreading the Gospel of salvation in Christ Jesus.

# Prayer # 3 – Acts 6:1-4; 7:1-53; 10:1-2; 12:1-8

Lord I pray that the level of organization and administration that existed in the early church be demonstrated in our local church. Let those who are called to preach the Word, give themselves continually to prayer and to the ministry of the Word, and others, to the business of ministration. Lord, rise up and appoint men and women, who are full of the Holy Ghost and wisdom, to serve in this ministry.

Father, I thank You that You had planned my redemption and restoration from the beginning of creation, and through the lives of prophets, You have paved the way for the fulfillment of your promise. From the promise to Abraham and his seed to the twelve patriarchs, who sold Joseph into prison, to whom you gave favor and wisdom, in the sight of Pharaoh; to Moses the ruler and deliverer, who was sent to deliver Your people from under the bondage of the Egyptians; Moses testifying of a prophet that You would rise up unto his brethren, and Him shall they hear. This prophet was You, our Lord and Savior Jesus Christ.

Like Cornelius, help me to be a devoted Christian who is walking in the fear of the Lord and living a life of giving and prayer.

Lord the apostles and early believers demonstrated the power of prayer in their daily walk. They never failed to approach You in prayer concerning every situation and trouble they encountered. Help me today Father to return to prayer. Let prayer be the distinguishing mark of everything that I do. Help me to seek You in prayer for everything and in everything.

# Prayer # 4 – Acts 16:5, 16 – 34; 17:10 – 28; 18:1 – 21; 24:24

O Father let the church continue to be established in the faith and increase in number daily.

Father, whatever situation I am facing, I am committing to prayer and praise. These were the weapons used by Paul and Silas, to shake the foundations of the prison they were in. Father I speak to every obstacle in my life that has me imprisoned. I command every door to be opened and every band to be loosed, in the name of Jesus. Lord what the enemy meant for my bad, turn it around for Your good, so that Your purposes are accomplished in the midst of my trials.

Lord, let those who are not saved receive the Word with all readiness of mind and searched the scriptures daily, so that they might believe and be saved. I pray against those who would want to stir up strife among the brethren, or lead the new believer astray. Watch over our new believers, Lord, and may they grow in the knowledge of the scriptures.

God my Father, You have made the world and all things therein. You are both Lord of the heaven and Lord of the earth. You do not dwell in temples made with hands. You are not worshipped with men's hands, as though You needed anything. Lord, You gave life to all, and breath to all things. Father, You have made of one blood, all nations of men, to dwell on all the face of the earth, and You have determined the times before appointed, and the bounds of their habitation so that men should seek You, and to find You, if haply they should feel after You; though You are not far from every one of us. Lord I confess that it is in You I live and move, and have my being. I am Your offspring.

Lord as you instructed Paul with these words, I declare

the same over my life. I declare that I will not be afraid but will speak and hold not my peace, for You are with me O Lord, and no man shall set on me to hurt me. You are my protection Lord.

Father, I give thanks for the Apostle Paul and his commitment to spreading the Gospel of Jesus, to the uttermost parts of the world. I thank you that he did not lose heart in the midst of the persecutions, but through Your grace and Holy Spirit, he was able to preach the Gospel of salvation in no other but Jesus Christ. He served with humility of mind; sometimes with many tears and temptations but he kept back nothing that was profitable to the saints. He showed them and taught them publicly, testifying both to the Jews and to the Greeks, repentance toward God, and faith toward the Lord Jesus Christ. Lord, grant unto me that same zeal in declaring the Gospel to a world that is wrapped in darkness. Help me to be dedicated in spreading the message of hope, deliverance, healing and restoration. Lord, Paul as he departed to Jerusalem to be bound, encouraged the Leaders that they take heed in feeding all the flock over which the Holy Spirit hath made them overseers. I pray his very instructions over our Pastors, Bishops and Elders may they feed the church of God which He has purchased with His own blood. Remind them O Lord, of this high call. I commend them to You Lord and to the Word of Your grace, which is able to build them up and to give them an inheritance among all them who are sanctified.

Like Paul Lord, help me to always exercise myself in having a good conscience void of offence towards God and towards men.

I thank you Father that through the ministry of Paul, salvation was brought to the Gentiles. I have heard it and I have believed it. I thank you Jesus. AMEN!

# Pauline Epistles:

*Praying*

# Romans

### Summary of the Book

In the book of Romans, the author Paul sets out the foundations of the Christian faith: all people are sinful, Christ died to forgive sin, and through faith we are made right with God. He gave practical guidelines for how the believer should behave and conduct oneself. Paul shows the insufficiency of just knowing the Word; we must let it transform our lives.

As you pray the book of Romans you will pray God's righteous rules for your life; denouncing the works of unrighteousness and lawlessness in and around you

## Let us Pray:
# Prayer # 1 – Romans 1:5 – 5:10

I thank you Father that through obedience to faith in Christ Jesus I have received grace and have been called of Jesus Christ.

I confess that I am not ashamed of the Gospel of Christ, for it is the power of God unto salvation to everyone that believes, and therein is the righteousness of God revealed, from faith to faith. The just shall live by faith.

Lord, let the wrath of God be revealed from heaven against all ungodliness and unrighteousness, in our community and in our nation; against all those who restrain the truth through their unrighteousness. Lord let indignation and wrath fall upon those who are contentious and do not obey the truth. Let tribulation and anguish be upon those who do evil. O, God, let glory, honor and peace be upon everyone that worketh good. Lord, help me to be a doer of the law so that I will be justified before You.

Lord, I confess and admit that there is no one righteous, and therefore, I am a sinner. I have sinned and have come short of the glory of God. Thank you Father, for having justified me freely by Your grace, through the redemption that is in Christ Jesus. Thank you for justifying me by faith without the deeds of the law. I thank you Father that my iniquities are forgiven, and my sins are covered through the blood of Jesus Christ. I thank you for imputing righteousness unto me, not by my works but through my faith in Christ Jesus. Blessed is the man to whom You will not impute sin. I thank you Father that I am made heir of Jesus Christ, through the righteousness of faith.

God our Father, You are the one who quickens the dead and calls those things which are not as though they were. Father, quicken every dead thing in and around me and called into being those things in my life, my church, my community which be not, as though they were.

Lord like Abraham; cause me to believe in hope against hope. Let me not be weak in faith, let me not stagger at any of the promise You have spoken over my life, through unbelief, but help me to be strong in faith, giving glory to Your name. Help me to be fully persuaded that what You have promised, You are well able to perform.

Father I believe in You, who raised Jesus Christ our Lord from the dead. He was delivered for our offenses, and was raised again for our justification. Thank you Father that I have peace with You through my Lord Jesus Christ because of my justification by faith.

Lord, I rejoice in the hope of the glory of God who has given me access by faith into this grace that I stand. Help me therefore to glory in tribulation, knowing that tribulation worketh patience and patience experience, and experience hope. Hope is that which makes me not ashamed because the love of God is shed abroad in my heart by the Holy Ghost.

Thank you again Jesus, for dying for me at the appropriate time. Thank you for commending Your love towards me that while I was yet a sinner you died for me. Thank you for saving me from wrath through your shed blood. Amen!

## Prayer # 2 – Romans 5:11 – 8:30

O God, I joy in You through our Lord Jesus Christ, by whom I have received atonement. Thank you God that through Christ's obedience, many were made righteous. Thank you for causing grace to abound towards me. I thank you Father that my old man was crucified with Christ, and therefore sin is destroyed in my body, and henceforth I will not serve sin. For he that is dead, is free from sin. I am dead unto sin but alive unto God, through Jesus Christ, my Lord.

I declare that no sin will reign in my body that I should obey it, in the lust thereof. I will not yield my members as instruments of unrighteousness unto sin, but I will yield myself unto God, and my members as instruments of righteousness. Sin shall have no dominion over me, for I am not under law but under grace. Lord I choose to yield my members as servants to righteousness, unto holiness. I thank you Father for the gift of eternal life through Jesus Christ my Lord.

Father, may I serve You in the newness of the Spirit and not in the oldness of the letter. Lord, I come against any law in my member that is warring against the law of my mind, and bringing me into captivity, to the law of sin. Deliver me from this body of death, through Jesus Christ my Lord.

Father, I choose to walk after the Spirit and not after the flesh. I come against every condemnation from the enemy. There is no condemnation to them who are in Christ Jesus, who walks not after the flesh, but after the Spirit. Father I thank you that "the law of the Spirit of life in Christ Jesus, has made me free from the law of sin and death."

Lord, deliver me from a carnal mind, and help me to be spiritually minded, so that I can enjoy life and peace, and not death. Forgive me Father, if I have been walking in the flesh.

The flesh cannot please You, and so I will choose to walk in the Spirit.

Father, quicken my mortal body by Christ's Spirit that lives in me. I choose to mortify the deeds of the body through the Spirit so that I may live.

I confess that I am a son of God and have received the Spirit of adoption. I am an heir of God and a joint heir with Christ Jesus.

I thank you Father that the sufferings of this present time, are not worthy to be compared with the glory which shall be revealed in me. O God, Your creation waits in expectation for the manifestation of the sons of God.

Father, I thank you for the hope I have in Christ Jesus. Help me to wait patiently for this hope. I thank you Holy Spirit for helping me in my intercession, with groaning which cannot be uttered. Holy Spirit, search my heart and intercede for me, according to the will of God.

Lord, I am confident that "all things work together for good, to those who love You and are called according to Your purpose." Thank you that I am predestined, called, justified and glorified. In Jesus' name, Amen!

# Prayer # 3 – Romans 8:31 – 39; 11:33 – 36; 12:1 – 16:20

Lord, if You are for me, who can be against me. You, O God, who spared not Your own Son but delivered Him up for us all, shall also with Him, give us all things freely. Lord, I come against those who will lay any charge against Your elect, or who condemns. I declare that nothing shall separate me from the love of Christ. No tribulation, distress, persecution, famine, or nakedness; no peril or sword; not even death nor life; not angels nor principalities; no powers or things present; nor things to come; not height or depth; nothing, by no means, shall be able to separate me from the love of God, which I have in Christ Jesus. I am more than a conqueror through Christ who loves me.

Father, I confess with my mouth, the Lord Jesus and I believe in my heart that You raise Him from the dead. Thank you that I shall not be ashamed because I believe in Christ.

O Father, "the depth of the riches of Your wisdom and knowledge. Your judgments are unsearchable and Your ways are past finding out." Lord no one knows Your mind; neither hath anyone being Your counselor. "For in You and through You and to You, are all things. To You O Lord belongs the glory forever."

Lord, You have been merciful to me and so by Your mercy, I choose to present my body to You as a living sacrifice, holy and acceptable. This is my reasonable act of worship and service. I choose not to conform to this present world but to be transformed by the renewing of my mind. Lord through the grace given unto to me, I choose not to think of myself more highly than I ought to think but I will think soberly, according to the measure of faith that God had dealt to me.

Lord, let my love be without dissimulation, and help me to abhor that which is evil, and cleave to that which is good. Help me Spirit of God to be kindly affectionate to others with brotherly love; in honor preferring others. Help me not to be slothful in business. Forgive me for the times I have been. Help me to remain fervent in spirit, serving the Lord. Let me rejoice always in hope, patient in tribulation, and continuing instant in prayer. Help me to distribute to the necessity of the saints. Let me give myself to hospitality. Lord, help me to bless those who persecute me and not to curse them. Forgive me for the times I have cursed them instead of blessing them.

I will rejoice with those who rejoice, and weep with those who weep. Help me Father to be of the same mind toward others. Let me not mind high things but be contented with men of low estate or with mean things. Help me never to become wise in my own conceit, nor recompense to any evil for evil. Let me provide things honest in the sight of all men. Father, help me to live peaceably with all men. Help me not to avenge myself. Instead if my enemy hunger may I feed him; if he thirsts may I give him drink. Help me not to be overcome of evil but to overcome evil with good.

Father, I pray against the rulers who have become terrors to good works; against those who fail to execute judgment upon those who do evil; against those who waste the resources of your people when they obediently pay over their taxes. Father I will give fear unto whom fear is due and honor to those whom honor is due.

Lord, You said I must owe no man anything but to love him. Help me to love everyone whom I come in contact with. For if I love, I have fulfilled the law. I will not commit adultery; nor kill; nor steal; nor bear false witness. I will not covet. I will instead love my neighbor as I love myself. I cast off every work of darkness and I put on the armor of light. I will walk honestly, not in rioting and drunkenness; not in strife and envying but I will put on the Lord Jesus Christ. I will make no provision for the flesh to fulfill the lusts thereof.

Lord, forgive me for the times I have judged my brother. Let me not put a stumbling block or an occasion to fall in my brother's way. Help me to walk charitably toward the brethren.

Lord, the Kingdom we are called to, the Kingdom of God, is not meat and drink but it is righteousness, peace and joy in the Holy Ghost. Help me to serve You Christ in all these things: righteousness, peace and joy. I will follow after the things which make for peace and the things that will edify others.

Father, for those of us who are strong believers, may we bear the infirmities of the weak and not seek after pleasing ourselves but to please our neighbors; for his good to edification.

Lord I praise You and I laud You. In You I put my trust. O God of hope, I'm asking You to fill me with all joy and peace in believing that I may abound in hope, through the power of the Holy Ghost.

Lord, fill me with goodness and all knowledge, so that I will be able to admonish others.

Help me Lord to avoid those who cause divisions and offences, contrary to the doctrine which we have learnt. Help me to walk in obedience. Help me to be wise unto that which is good, and simple, concerning evil. God of peace, bruise Satan under our feet and may the grace of Jesus Christ be with us.

Now to Him that is of power to establish me according to the gospel and preaching of Jesus Christ; according to the revelation of the mystery which was kept secret since the world began; but is made manifest, and by the scriptures of the prophets. According to the commandments of the everlasting God, made known to all nations, for the obedience of the faith: To God only wise be glory through Jesus Christ, forever, Amen!

*Praying*

# 1 Corinthians

## Summary of the Book

The purpose of the book of 1 Corinthians, addresses the problems the Corinthians were facing. The Christians in Corinth were struggling with their environment. Surrounded by corruption and every conceivable sin, they felt pressured to adapt. We face the same challenges and struggles today. Paul encouraged them, by first, addressing the problems of division and disorder within the church. He taught on Christian marriage, Christian freedom, public worship and Jesus' resurrection.

As you pray Corinthians you will come to appreciate unity and order in your local church and the body of Christ. You will develop greater commitment to living a life directed by the Spirit of God.

## Let us Pray:
# Prayer # 1 – 1 Corinthians 1:3 – 3:23

Father, grant unto me grace by Jesus Christ that in everything I am enriched by Him; in all utterance, and in all knowledge; so that I come behind in no gift; waiting on Christ, who will confirm me until the end. Faithful are You Lord, who have called me unto fellowship with Christ Jesus.

Help me Father, to preserve the unity of the saints. Let there be no division in my relations to others. Help me to speak the same thing and to be perfectly joined together in thought and judgment.

Lord, I accept Christ and the gospel, as the power of God, and the wisdom of God. The foolishness of God is wiser that man's wisdom, and the weakness of God, is stronger than man's strength. Thank you Father, for choosing the foolish things of the world to confound the wise, and for choosing the weak things of the world, to confound the things which are mighty. Therefore, no flesh shall glory in your presence. I declare that Christ Jesus is my wisdom, my righteousness, my sanctification, and my redemption. Father, I glory not in my own strength or abilities, but I glory in the Lord Jesus Christ who is all in all.

I am determined, to know only Jesus Christ, and Him crucified, and nothing else. Father cause those who are entrusted with the preaching of the Gospel to do so, not with enticing words of men's wisdom, but in demonstration of the Spirit, and of power that others faith, stand not in the wisdom of men, but in the power of God.

I thank you Father, for the hidden wisdom, which You ordained before the world, unto our glory, and revealing unto us by Your Spirit, the things that were hidden from men of old. Thank you, for revealing unto us the things that God hath prepared for those who love Him. You have revealed them unto us by Your Spirit; for the Spirit searches all things, yea the deep things of God. Thank you for giving me the Holy Spirit that I might know the things that are freely given to me.

I declare that I have the mind of Christ. The natural man receives not the things of the Spirit of God, for they are foolishness unto him; neither can he know them because they are spiritually discerned. But I thank you Father that I have the mind of Christ.

Lord, help me to walk in the Spirit that I might be able to discern the things that are spiritual. Lord, remove from me any trace of envying, strife or divisions, because these things are carnal and are not traits of those who are spiritual.

I declare, that I am a co-laborer with God. I am God's husbandry and God's building. My body is the temple of God, and the Spirit of God dwells in me.

Father, help me not to walk, according to this world's wisdom because the wisdom of this world is foolishness unto You. Help me not to glory in men, for all things are ours, and we are Christ's, and Christ is God's. Amen!

# Prayer # 2 – 1 Corinthians 4:6 – 20; 6:1 – 10:12

Lord, may You find me a faithful steward. Help me not to judge anything before the time, until You come to bring light to the hidden things of darkness, and manifest the counsels of the hearts. Then shall every man praise You. Help me Holy Spirit, not to think of men above that which is written, so that no one becomes puffed up against another. Help me to walk before You and others in humbleness of heart and mind. Your Kingdom Lord is not in word but in power.

Lord, remove from me any offence to your name: fornication, malice, wickedness, and help me to walk in sincerity and truth. O Lord, be glorified in my body, and in my spirit.

I thank you Lord that having walked as unrighteous, I have now been washed, sanctified and justified in the name of the Lord Jesus, and by the Spirit of God. The unrighteous shall not inherit the Kingdom of God.

All things are lawful unto me, but all things are not expedient; all things are lawful for me, but I will not be brought under the power of any. Father, I acknowledge that my body is the member of Christ, and so I will not take my members and make them the members of a harlot. God forbid. My body is the temple of the Holy Ghost. I have been bought with a price and will therefore glorify God in my body and in my spirit; which are God's.

Lord, help me not to walk according to knowledge because knowledge puffs up. Instead, help me to walk in love, because love edifies. I confess that there is but One God, the Father of whom are all things; and one Lord Jesus Christ, by whom are all things, and we are in Him. Father, help me not to use my liberty to become a stumbling block to those who are weak. I know that meat commends us, not to You. If we eat, we are not better, and if we do not eat, are we worst but let me not use my knowledge to cause my weak brother to stumble.

`Father, may those who plough, plough in hope, and those that thresh in hope, be partakers of this hope. Lord, those who preach the gospel are to live of the gospel. I pray against those who would abuse their power of reward by preaching the Gospel with charge.

Like Paul, Father, help me to be made all things to all men that I might by all means save some. Help me not to cause an offence in preaching the Gospel. Help me Father to run the race set before me, with the intention of winning the prize. May I keep my body under and bring it unto subjection, so that I do not become a cast away.

Help me Holy Spirit, not to lust after evil things, or be an idolater, nor commit fornication, nor tempt Christ, nor murmur, as the Israelites did in the wilderness. Help me to take heed lest I think I stand, I fall. Amen!

# Prayer # 3- 1 Corinthians 11:2 – 12:31

Thank you O God, for Your faithfulness not to suffer me, to be tempted above that which I am able to bear, but with the temptation, will make a way of escape for me. Father, in all I do, may I do it to the glory of Your name, and not causing any offense to others. All things are lawful for me but not all things are expedient. All things are lawful for me but all things edify not.

I declare that the earth is the Lord's and the fullness thereof. Lord, I pray that You will restore divine order in our homes, where the man is subjected to You as his head, and the woman is subjected to her husband, as her head. In like manner, as You Christ is subjected to God the Father as Your head. Let the man reflect the image and glory of God, and let the woman reflect the glory of the man. The man was not created for the woman but the woman for the man. Help our women to come into knowledge of their position, in Your divine order of creation, as well as the men. Let neither abuse their purpose because neither is the man without the woman in the Lord, and neither is the woman without the man.

Lord Jesus, I thank you, for Your body, which was broken for me, and for the new testament in Your blood. Help me Spirit of the living God, not to eat the bread and drink of the Lord's cup unworthily, and thereby becoming guilty of the blood of the Lord; not discerning the Lord's body.

Lord, thank you, for the diversities of gifts, the differences of administrations, and the diversities of operations in the Church. Though they are diverse and different, You are the same God, Lord and Spirit, which works all in all. Help us Holy Spirit, to use the manifestations to profit all. I thank you for the gifts: word of wisdom, word of knowledge, faith, gifts of healing, working of miracles, prophecy, discerning of spirits, divers kinds of tongues and the interpretation of tongues. Let these gifts be evident in the operation of the life of the church as well as in my life.

Lord, I acknowledge that we are one body, but many members, and none of us can say we can do without the other members. Remove from us O Lord, schisms and divisions in the body, and help us to have the same care one for another. Help us to share in the sufferings and joy of others, as members of one body. Help us to operate each in our gifts. In Jesus' name, Amen!

# Prayer # 4 – 1 Corinthians 13:1 – 16:14

Spirit of the Living God, teach me to walk in love. The love that suffers long is kind and does not envy; love that is not rash nor puffed up; love that does not behave itself unseemingly or seeks her own; love that is not easily provoked or thinks evil; love that rejoices not in iniquity but rejoices in the truth. The love that bears all things, believes all things, hope all things, and endure all things. Holy Spirit I want this love that never fails. Prophecy shall fail. Tongues shall cease. Knowledge shall vanish away, but love shall never fail. There abides faith, hope, and love, but the greatest of these, is love. May I follow after charity, and desire spiritual gifts that will edify the church. Help me O God, not to be a child in understanding but like men.

Guard me O Lord from evil communication, because evil communication corrupts good manners. I thank you Lord, for the promise of the resurrection. All thanks are unto You Father, who gives us the victory through our Lord Jesus Christ. I will remain steadfast, unmovable, always abounding in the work of the Lord, knowing that my labor is not in vain. I will stand fast in the faith, and be strong. I will do all things in love. In Jesus name I pray, Amen!

*Praying*

# 11 Corinthians

## Summary of the Book

In the book of Second Corinthians, Paul wrote to help the Christians in Corinth with specific moral issues that were present in the church and to answer questions on sex, marriage and tender consciences. Most Christians received Paul's first letter, but there were false teachers who denied Paul's authority. Paul therefore wrote second Corinthians to defend his character and authority, and to explain the nature of the Christian ministry.

As you pray Second Christians, you will embrace Paul's words of love and encouragement. You will affirm your commitment to the truth of God's Word and reject false teaching

# Prayer # 1 – 11 Corinthians 1:3 – 4; 20 – 22; 2:14 – 4:18

Blessed be God, the Father of our Lord Jesus Christ, the Father of all mercies, and the God of all comfort; who comforts us in all our tribulation that we may be able to comfort them, who are in trouble.

I thank you God for establishing me in Christ, and anointing me, and giving me the earnest of the Spirit in my heart.

Father, help my leaders to uphold righteousness and purity, by disciplining those who cause offence. Help them also, to forgive and comfort, and encourage these persons; to keep them from being overwhelmed by excessive sorrow and despair. Let them assure others of Your love.

Lord, I thank you that You always cause me to triumph in Christ. Spread through me, O Lord, and make evident the fragrance of the knowledge of God everywhere. Let my life be a sweet fragrance of Christ unto You Father.

Lord, my sufficiency is in You. I thank you for the ministration of the Spirit which is more glorious than the ministration of death. Thank you Father that the Spirit gives life. You, O Lord, are that Spirit, and where the Spirit of the Lord is, there is liberty. Help me to be changed from glory to glory, even as by the Spirit of the Lord.

Father, may the light of the glorious gospel of Christ, the image of God, shine upon the hearts of those whose minds are blinded by the god of this world. Let them be able to walk in the truth that is able to set them free.

Father, I renounce dishonesty, craftiness, and everything

that would cause me to handle the Word of God deceitfully. Let me preach, not of myself, but Christ Jesus the Lord. May I recognize myself as a mere servant of Jesus.

Lord, I thank you for shining in my heart, and giving me the light of the knowledge of the glory of God, in the face of Jesus Christ. Help me O God, not to faint in my afflictions and distresses. Though the outward man perishes, yet my inward man is renewed day by day. Help me not to look on the things which are seen, but at the things which are not seen; for the things that are seen are temporal, but the things which are not seen, are eternal. Amen!

## Prayer #2 – 11 Corinthians 5:1 – 9:15

Thank you Father, for giving unto us the earnest of the Spirit. We are therefore always confident that while we are at home in the body, we are absent from the Lord but to be absent from the body, is to be present with the Lord. Whether we are absent or present, may we be accepted by You.

Help me O God, to walk by faith and not by sight. Father, may I live for Christ, who died for me and rose again. Thank you that in Christ Jesus, I am a new creature, old things are passed away behold all things have become new. Thank you for reconciling me Father to Yourself, through Jesus Christ, and have given unto me the ministry of reconciliation. I am therefore an ambassador for Christ. Father, You made Christ sin for us, who knew no sin that I might be made the righteousness of God in Him. I Thank you Father.

Father, I receive not the grace of God in vain. Like the Apostles, help me in all things to approve myself as a minister of God: in patience, in afflictions, in necessities, in distresses, in stripes, in imprisonments, in tumults, in watching, in fasting; by pureness, by knowledge, by longsuffering, by kindness, by the Holy Ghost, by unfeigned love, by the Word of truth, by the power of the God, by the armor of righteousness, by honor and dishonor, by evil report and good report......... as sorrowful, yet always rejoicing, as poor, yet making many rich; as having nothing but possessing all things.

Father, I come against any fellowship in this body with unrighteousness or any communion with darkness. I will not be unequally yoke with unbelievers. I am the temple of the living God. God dwells in me. He is my God, and I am His child. I separate myself from every form of unrighteousness, darkness, idols and infidels. Be a Father unto me O God. I cleanse myself from all filthiness in the flesh and spirit. Let me be perfected in holiness in the fear of God.

Lord, give me godly sorrow that leads to repentance. Help me to abound in everything, in faith and utterance, in knowledge and all diligence, and in love for the brethren. Thank you Father, that Jesus Christ, Thou he was rich, for our sake, He became poor that we through His poverty, might become rich.

Lord, I purpose in my heart, to give not grudgingly, or of necessity but cheerfully, because Christ loves a cheerful giver. Lord, as I give, let Your grace abound toward me that having sufficiency in all things, I will be able to abound to every good work. Father, You who minister seed to the sower, minster bread for my food and multiply the seeds I have sown and increase the fruits of my righteousness. Cause me to be enriched in everything, in all bountifulness. Thank you Lord for Your unspeakable gift. Amen!

# Prayer # 3 – 11 Corinthians 10:1 – 13:14

Father, thou I am in the flesh, I do not war after the flesh. The weapons of my warfare are not carnal but are mighty through God, to the pulling down of strongholds; the casting down of imaginations and every high thing that exalts itself against the knowledge of God, and bringing into captivity, every thought, to the obedience of Christ.

Father, I glory in You. Like the apostle Paul, let me glory in my infirmities that the power of Christ may rest upon me. Indeed, Your grace is sufficient for me and You strength is made perfect in my weakness. For when I am weak, You are strong.

Help me Father, to be perfect, to be of good comfort, to be of one mind, and to live in peace. Let the love of God and His peace be with me. Let the grace of the Lord Jesus Christ, the love of God and the communion of the Holy Ghost be with me. Amen!

*Praying*

# Galatians

### Summary of the Book

The book of Galatians is referred as the charter of Christian freedom. In this book Paul proclaims the reality of our liberty in Christ – freedom from the law and the power of sin and freedom to serve the living God

As you pray these Scriptures, allow the freedom that God has brought to you, through Jesus Christ, resonate in your life. You are no longer bound, you are free. Free to live, free to love and free to give.

## Let us Pray:
# Prayer # 1 – Galatians 1:1 – 6:10

Thank you Jesus for giving Yourself for my sins, and for delivering me from this present evil world, in accordance to the will of God my Father, to whom belongs glory forever and ever.

Father, I confess that I am crucified with Christ, and it is no longer I that lives, but Christ who lives in me. The life I now live in this body, I live by faith in the Son of God, who loved me, and gave himself up for me.

Father, help me to live by faith because it is the people who live by faith, who are the true sons of Abraham, and who are blessed and favored by God. Father, I believe that I am justified by faith, and not by obedience to the law. I will therefore live by and out of faith.

I thank you Christ, for purchasing my freedom from the curse of the law, and its condemnation, by being a curse for me. I thank you, for making me a son; an heir of the promise. We are all children of God by faith in Christ Jesus. And if we be Christ's, then are we Abraham's seed and heirs according to the promise.

I declare that I am a son of God. I am an heir of God through Jesus Christ. I will stand fast in the liberty where Christ has made me free and will not become entangled again with the yoke of bondage.

I thank you Father, for calling me unto liberty. I will not use my freedom as an opportunity or excuse for selfishness, but to serve others, through love. Father, I commit to love my neighbor as myself. I will walk and live in the Spirit, so that I will not gratify the cravings and desires of the flesh.

Father, I come against any workings of the flesh in my body. I come against immorality, indecency, idolatry, sorcery, enmity, strife, jealousy, anger, selfishness, divisions, envy and drunkenness. Fill me O Father with the fruit of the Holy Spirit. Fill me with love, joy, peace, patience, kindness, goodness, faithfulness, gentleness and self-control. Remove from me vainglory, self-conceit, competitive and challenging behavior towards others. Help me to walk and live by the Holy Spirit.

Father, I pray as well, for those who may have been overtaken by sin, that we, who are mature, will restore and reinstate them back into faith, with all gentleness. Help us to bear each others' burden. Lord, help me not to lose heart, and grow weary and faint, in acting nobly and doing right; for in due time, at the appointed season, I shall reap. Help me to do good to all people as the opportunity arises. Let me be a blessing to those of the household of faith. (AMP)

Father I will glory in nothing except in the cross of our Lord Jesus Christ. Amen!

*Praying*

# Ephesians

### Summary of the Book

The book of Ephesians is a letter of encouragement sent by the Apostle Paul to the Gentile churches in Asia. The major theme is, the church is the body of Christ and each part must work as a unit, with Christ being the head.

As you pray the book of Ephesians, allow the purpose of God for His church to become your mission. As you pray, your spirit will become submissive to the will of Christ, and you will develop a greater desire to love others.

**Let us Pray:**

# Prayer # 1 – Ephesians 1:3 – 2:10 (AMP)

All blessings, praise and laudation, be to the God and Father of our Lord Jesus Christ; who has blessed me with every spiritual blessing, in the heavenly realm.

Thank you Father, for choosing me in Christ before the foundation of the world, to be holy, consecrated, and set a part for You, and blameless in Your sight. I thank you Father, that You have planned in love for me, to be adopted as Your own child through Jesus Christ, in accordance with the purpose of Your will; so that I might be to the praise and commendation of Your glorious grace. Lord, in You I have redemption through Your blood, the forgiveness of offences, in accordance with the riches and the generosity of Your gracious favor. In You Lord, I was made God's heritage, and I have obtained an inheritance. Father I have been destined and appointed to live for the praise of Your glory.

I thank you for the Holy Spirit, our sealed promise, and also the guarantee of our inheritance.

Father, grant unto me the Spirit of wisdom and revelation, in the knowledge of You. Let the eyes of my heart flood with light, so that I can know and understand, the hope to which You have called me, and how rich is Your glorious inheritance in the saints. Help me Father to know the immeasurable and unlimited, and surpassing greatness of your power in, and for us, who believe.

I thank you Lord that You in Your mercy, while I was yet a sinner, You made me alive together in fellowship, and in union with Christ. Thank you, for saving me by Your grace, favor and mercy, I did not deserve. Thank you, for raising me up together with Christ, and made me to sit down together in the heavenly sphere, in Christ Jesus, the Messiah, the Anointed One. Lord, how immeasurable is the riches of Your unmerited favor in Your kindness and goodness of heart towards us in Christ Jesus. I declare that I am God's own handiwork, His workmanship, recreated in Christ Jesus, to do good works, which God predestined for me that I should walk in them. Amen!

# Prayer # 2 – Ephesians 2:14 – 3:21 (AMP)

Lord, You are my peace. You have made us, both Jews and Gentiles, one body, and have broken down the hostile dividing wall between us. We are no longer outsiders, excluded from the rights of citizens, but now share citizenship with the saints; God's own people, consecrated and set apart for Himself. We are built upon the foundation of the apostles and prophets, with Christ Jesus himself, the chief cornerstone. In Him whom the whole structure is joined together harmoniously, and which continues to grow and increase, into a holy temple; a sanctuary dedicated, consecrated, and sacred to the presence of God.

I am now a fellow heir, a member of the same body, and joint partaker in the same divine promise in Christ, through the Gospel. Thank you Father, for the boldness of free access to You, because of my faith in Christ Jesus.

O Father, of our Lord Jesus Christ, for whom every family in heaven and on earth is named, grant unto me, out of the rich treasury of Your glory, to be strengthened and reinforced with mighty power, in my inner man, by the Holy Spirit. Let Christ dwell in my heart. May I be rooted deep in love, and be found securely on love. May I have the power, and be strong to grasp the breadth, length, height, and depth of Your love. Help me Lord to come to know the love of Christ, which surpasses mere knowledge. Let me be filled with the fullness of God.

Unto You O God, by the power that is at work within me, who is able to do super-abundantly, far over, and above all, that I dare ask or think; to you be glory in the church and in Christ Jesus throughout all generations, forever and ever. Amen!

# Prayer # 3 – Ephesians 4:1 – 5:11 (AMP)

Help me Holy Spirit to walk worthy of the vocation to which I have been called. Help me to walk with lowliness and meekness, with longsuffering, forbearing with others in love. Help me to always endeavor to keep the unity of the Spirit, in the bond of peace.

O God, You are the Father who is above all, and through all, and in us all.

Thank you, for the grace given to me, according to the measure of the gift of Christ. I thank you, for the gift of the Apostle, the gift of the Prophet, the Evangelist, the Pastor, and the Teacher; given to us for the perfecting of the saints, for the work of the ministry, and for the edifying of the Body. Help me Holy Spirit to know my gift, so that I can play my part that all will come in the unity of the faith, and in the knowledge of the Son of God. To come into the fullness of Christ and that we do not become carried about with every wind of doctrine, but be able to speak the truth in love, and grow to maturity into Christ, in all things.

Father, I will not walk in the vanity of my mind but will put off the old man, which is corrupt. I will instead, be renewed in the spirit of my mind, by putting on the new man, which is created in righteousness, and true holiness. I therefore, put away lying, anger, stealing, corrupt communication, all bitterness, wrath, clamor and malice. I take unto myself truth – I will speak truth to my neighbors. I will not allow the sun to go down on my wrath. I will not give place to the devil. I will engage in honest labor. I will engage in communication that will edify and minister grace to the hearers. Lord, I will be kind to others, tender-hearted, and forgiving; even as You have forgiven me.

I choose and commit, to be a follower of God. I choose and commit, to walk in love, as Christ has loved me, and has given himself for me. An offering and a sacrifice to God, as a sweet smelling savor. I will not engage in fornication, uncleanness or covetousness, neither filthiness, nor foolish talking, nor jesting. I will rather engage in the giving of thanks. I will walk as a child of light. Let the Holy Spirit produce in me a life of goodness, righteousness and truth.

Father, in the name of Jesus, I reprove the unfruitful works of darkness, and will have no fellowship with them. Amen!

# Prayer # 4 – Ephesians 5:15 – 6:8 (AMP)

Help me Holy Spirit, to walk circumspectly, not as fool but as wise. Help me, to redeem the time because the days are truly evil. Help me to understand what the will of the Lord is. Fill me O God, with thy Spirit; may I speak to others in psalms, hymns and spiritual songs; may I give thanks to You always, in and for all things, in the name of our Lord Jesus Christ.

Lord, remember all my relationships. Help me to submit to others in the fear of God.

**For wives:** Help me as a wife to submit myself to my husband as unto the Lord. Help me to recognize that my husband is the head of me, even as Christ is the head of the Church, and the Savior of the Body. Help my husband to love me, even as You also loved the Church and gave Yourself for it; that You might sanctify and cleanse it, with the washing of water by the Word, and presenting it to Yourself a glorious Church; not having spot or wrinkle, or any such thing, but is holy and without blemish. May my husband nourish and cherish me as his own flesh, even as Christ the Church. I pray for the spiritual, emotional, financial and social unity of my husband; may we become one flesh.

**For husbands:** Help my wife to submit herself to me as unto the Lord. Help her to recognize that I am her head, even as Christ is the head of the Church and the Savior of the Body. Help me to love her, even as You also loved the Church and gave Yourself for it; that You might sanctify and cleanse it with the washing of water by the word; presenting it to Yourself a glorious Church, not having spot or wrinkle or any such thing but is holy and without blemish. May I nourish and cherish her as my own flesh, even as Christ the Church. I pray for the spiritual, emotional, financial and social unity of my wife; may we become one flesh.

**For Parents:** Lord, may my children obey me in the Lord, for this is right in Your sight. Help them to honor us as their father and mother, that it may be well with them, and that they may live long on the earth. Help me as a father/mother not to provoke my children to wrath but instead bring them up in the nurture and admonition of the Lord.

Holy Spirit, help me to work as unto the Lord, and not as men pleasers. Help me to respect those who are my superiors; doing the will of God from the heart; knowing that whatsoever good I do, it shall be received of the Lord. In Jesus' name, Amen!

# Prayer # 5 – Ephesians 6:10 – 19 (AMP)

Father, I choose to remain strong in the Lord and in the power of His might. I will put on the whole armor of God, so that I will be able to stand against the evil-doings of the devil. I will stand having my loins girt about with truth, and having on the breastplate of righteousness. I will stand with my feet shod with the preparation of the Gospel of peace. I will stand, taking the shield of faith, to quench all the fiery darts of the wicked. I will stand, with the helmet of salvation, and the sword of the Spirit. I will stand, in prayer, with all perseverance and supplication for all saints.

Lord, I pray for those entrusted in preaching the Gospel, that utterance is given to them, and that they will speak boldly the mystery of the Gospel.

O God let Your grace be with them that love You and our Lord Jesus Christ in sincerity. Amen!

*Praying*

# Philippians

## Summary of the Book

The book of Philippians is a book of joy. When you read the book of Philippians you experience deep expressions of joy and the instruction to rejoice as believers. The main verse in this book is "Rejoice in the Lord always and again I say rejoice." The Apostle Paul encourages the believer to rejoice no matter what the circumstances of one's life, to be contented, to know Christ, and to obey Him.

As you pray the book of Philippians, follow Paul's goal to know Christ more. Rededicate yourself to finding joy that comes only in Christ Jesus. As you pray, you will experience joy in serving, joy in believing, joy in giving and joy in suffering.

## Let us Pray:
# Prayer # 1 – Philippians 1:5 – 2:15

Father, I thank you that You who hath begun a good work in me, shall complete it until the day of Jesus Christ. Father, let my love abound more and more, in knowledge and all judgment, so that I will approve all things that are excellent that I may be sincere and without offence, until the day of Christ. Cause me to be filled with the fruits of righteousness, which are by Jesus Christ, unto the praise and Glory of God.

Father I declare that "I shall not disgrace myself nor be put to shame in anything. I declare that Christ will be magnified and get the glory and praise in this body of mine and be boldly exalted in my person" (AMP). To live, for me is Christ, and to die is gain. Holy Spirit, help me to stand firm in "one Spirit and with one mind; striving together for the faith of the Gospel." I will not be terrified by my adversaries.

Father, I thank you for the consolation I have in Christ, the comfort of His love, the fellowship of His Spirit, and the bowels of His mercy. Help me Spirit of God, to have that same love, to be in accord, and one mind with the brethren. Remove from me strife and vainglory. Help me in the true Spirit of humility and lowliness of mind, to esteem others as better than me. Help me not to be concerned only for my own interest, but also for the interest of others. Let the same mind which was in Christ Jesus be in me. He thought it not robbery be to be equal with God, but made Himself of no reputation, and took upon Himself the form of a servant, and was made in the likeness of men; humbled Himself, and became obedient to death. Whereby, God has highly exalted Him, and has given Him a name that is above every name, that at the name of Jesus, every knee should bow, and every tongue should confess, that He is

Lord, to the glory of God the Father.

Father, work out in me the power, and the desire, both to will, and to do Your good pleasure. Help me Holy Spirit, to do things without murmuring and doubtful reasoning; so that I will be blameless and harmless; a child of God, without rebuke, in the midst of this crooked and perverse generation.

## Prayer # 2 – Philippians 3:1 – 4:19

Father, I will rejoice in the Lord. I will worship You in the Spirit and will rejoice in Christ Jesus. I will put no confidence in my flesh. Father like Paul, I count everything as loss, compared to the excellence of the knowledge of Christ Jesus my Lord, so that I might be found in Him, not having my own righteousness, but possessing righteousness which comes through faith in Christ.

Lord, I want to know Christ, and the power of His resurrection, and the fellowship of His sufferings, and to become conformed unto His death. Forgetting those things which are behind, I press on, toward the goal for the prize of the high calling of God, in Christ Jesus.

I will rejoice in you Lord. I will delight and gladden myself in You. I will not fret or have any anxiety about anything, but in every circumstance, and in everything by prayer and petition, with thanksgiving, I will make my wants known to God.

Whatever is true, whatever is honest, whatever is just, whatever is pure, whatever is lovely, whatever is of good report; if there is any virtue, any praise, I will think on those things.

Lord, help me to be content in whatever state I am. Help me to know both how to be abased and how to abound. I declare, that I can do all things through Christ who strengthens me. Help me to be a giver. Let my giving be a sacrifice, acceptable and well-pleasing to You. Lord as I give, may You supply all my needs according to Your riches in glory.

To You, our God and Father, let there be glory forever and ever, Amen.

*Praying*

# Colossians

## Summary of the Book

In the book of Colossians, Paul was writing to the Colossian church to combat the false teachers who were infiltrating the church. To combat the false teachings, Paul in the book, stressed the deity of Christ; looking closely at Christ's connection to the Father, and His sacrificial death on the cross for the sin of humanity. Everlasting life can only be achieved by connection with Christ through faith. Believers can only gain power for living the Christian life, by remaining connected to Christ.

As you pray Colossians you will settle your personal connection with Jesus Christ for salvation and power for living. You will gain a fresh appreciation for Christ as the fullness of God and the only source of living the Christian life.

## Let us pray:
# Prayer # 1 – Colossians 1:9 – 3:17 (AMP)

Father, I pray that You will cause me to be filled with the full knowledge of Your will, in all spiritual wisdom, and in understanding and discernment of spiritual things. Help me to walk in a manner worthy of the Lord, fully pleasing to Him in all things. Bearing fruit in every good work, and growing and increasing, in and by, the knowledge of God. Help me Father to be strengthened with all power, in order to exercise every kind of endurance and patience with joy.

I give You thanks Lord, for making me fit to share the portion which is the inheritance of the saints. Thank you Father for delivering and drawing me to Yourself, out of the control and the dominion of darkness, and has transferred me into the Kingdom of Your son Jesus Christ; in whom I have redemption through His blood.

Lord, You are the first born of all creation. In You all things were created, in heaven and on earth; things seen and unseen; thrones, dominion, rulers, and authorities. All things were created and they exist through You, and in, and for You. In You Lord, all things are held together. You are the head of the body, the church; the beginning, the firstborn from the dead that in all things You might have the pre-eminence. In You O Lord, shall all fullness dwell.

I thank you Jesus for reconciling me to God the Father, in the body of Your flesh, through death. As a result, I am holy, unblameable and unreprovable in Your sight. Help me Holy Spirit to walk in union with and conformity to Christ Jesus. Let the roots of my being, be firmly and deeply planted in Christ, and be continually built up in Him, so that I become established in the faith. In You O Lord, dwell all the fullness of the Godhead, and I am complete in You. I am buried with You in baptism and am thereby raised with You through the faith of the operation of God, who raised You from the dead. Lord, You have quickened me, and all my sins have been forgiven. I thank you Lord for blotting out the handwriting of ordinances that was against me, and nailing them on the cross.

Thank you Jesus for disarming the principalities and powers that was raged against me and triumphing over them on the cross.

Father, remove from me legalism, for I am dead with Christ and from the rudiments of the world and is therefore no longer subjected to them.

Father, I seek the eternal treasures that are above, where Christ is seated at Your right hand. I choose to set my mind and keep them set on what is above, not on things on the earth. Father I deprive of power every evil desire lurking in my body; sexual vice, impurity, sensual appetites, unholy desires and all greed and covetousness, anger, rage, bad feelings toward others, curses and slander, lying and foul-mouthed utterances. Father, I will instead clothe myself with behavior marked by tenderheartedness, mercy, gentle ways and patience. I will be gentle and fore-bearing with others; forgiving others, as the Lord has freely forgiven me. I put on love and enfold myself with the bond of perfectness and the peace from Christ shall rule in my heart. Lord whatever I do, in word or deed, I will do in the name of the Lord. Amen!

# Prayer # 2 – Colossians 3:18 – 4: 6 (AMP)

Lord I present the family to You, I pray that wives will submit themselves unto their husbands as it is fit in the Lord, and that husbands will love their wives and be not bitter against them. Let children be obedient to their parents in all things for this is well pleasing to You Lord. Let not fathers provoke their children to anger lest they become discouraged. Let those who are servants obey in all things their masters; not with eye service as men pleasers but in singleness of heart, fearing God. Lord, whatsoever we do, may we do it heartily as to the Lord and not unto men; knowing that we shall receive from You, the reward of the inheritance.

Help me Holy Spirit to continue in prayer, and be watchful in thanksgiving. I pray for those who are entrusted to preach the Gospel that God, You would open unto them a door of utterance to speak the mystery of Christ. Help me to walk in wisdom toward them that are without, redeeming the time. Let my speech be always with grace and seasoned with salt that I may know how I ought to answer every man. Let the Word of Christ have its home in my heart and mind and dwell in me in all its richness. Amen!

*Praying*

# 1 and 11 Thessalonians

### Summary of the Book

The books of Thessalonians offer assurance of Christ's return and the hope of the resurrection. In these books, believers are challenged to live a life that pleases the Lord, by avoiding sexual immorality; loving others and living as good citizens in a sinful world. There is a call to faithfulness and watchfulness in the book.

As you pray Thessalonians, you will reaffirm your hope in the reality of Jesus Christ's return, the resurrection and everlasting life.

# Prayer # 1 – 1 Thessalonians 1:1 – 5:11

I thank you Father, for grace and peace that comes from You and the Lord Jesus Christ. Thank you for entrusting me with the gospel. Help me to thereby speak, not as pleasing men but pleasing You; who tries my heart.

Help me Holy Spirit, to walk worthy of God, who has called me into His Kingdom and glory. Let the Word of God work effectually in me.

O Lord, make me to increase and abound in love towards all men. Establish my heart unblameable in holiness before God.

Help me Holy Spirit, to possess my vessel in sanctification and honor. This is God's will for me, my sanctification. Help me not to go beyond and defraud my brother or sister in any matter. Lord, You have not called me unto uncleanness but unto holiness. Let me increase more and more in brotherly love. Let me walk honestly towards them that are without and be not lacking of anything.

Help me Holy Spirit, to walk as a child of the light and not of darkness. Help me to be watchful and sober. I put on the breastplate of faith and love, and for a helmet, the hope of salvation. Thank you Father that you have not appointed me unto wrath, but to obtain salvation by our Lord Jesus Christ, who died for me that whether I wake or sleep, I shall live together with Him.

# Prayer # 2 – 1 Thessalonians 5:12 - 24

Father, I thank you for those who are over me in the Lord. Help me to esteem them highly in love for their work sake, and may we be at peace among ourselves. Lord I will follow that which is good. I will warn them that are disorderly. I will comfort the feeble minded. I will support the weak and I will be patient toward all men, by the help of the Holy Spirit, and the Lord Jesus Christ.

I choose O God to rejoice evermore; to pray without ceasing and to give thanks in everything. I will not quench the Spirit nor will I despite prophesying. I will prove all things and hold unto that which is good. I will abstain from all appearance of evil.

O God of peace, sanctify me wholly and may my whole spirit and soul and body be preserved blameless unto the coming of our Lord Jesus Christ. Amen!

# Prayer # 3 - II Thessalonians 1:3 – 3:18

Father, let my faith grow exceedingly and let my charity toward others abound. Help me to exercise patience and faith in all my tribulations. Recompense tribulation to them that trouble me O God my Father.

Father, may I be counted worthy of Your calling and may You fulfill all the good pleasure of Your goodness towards me. Let the name of the Lord Jesus Christ be glorified in me.

Guard my heart O Lord from deception as it relates to Your coming. Help me to walk in truth and have no pleasure in unrighteousness. I thank you Father for choosing me unto salvation through sanctification of the Spirit and belief of truth. I thank you for loving me and for giving me everlasting consolation, and good hope, through grace. May You comfort my heart and establish me in every good word, and work.

Father, I pray that the Word of the Lord will have free course and be glorified in the life of its hearers. Deliver those who preach the Word from unreasonable and wicked men, who have no faith. Lord, establish me and keep me from evil; direct my heart into the love of God and into the patient waiting of Christ. Help me not to become weary in well doing. Grant me your peace in Jesus name, Amen!

# Pastoral Epistles:

*Praying*

# 1 Timothy

### Summary of the book

The book of I Timothy offers insights and guidance for those in leadership. Paul wrote the book to Timothy, a young leader in the church at Ephesus. In this book Paul offers Timothy caring counsel, warning him of false teachers, urging him to hold on to his faith, giving practical counsel on pastoral care, and encouraging him to stand firm in the faith; and to live above reproach.

As you pray I Timothy, you will pray for your church leadership in line with the qualifications outlined in the book. You will confirm the importance of prayer and order in our worship and church services.

## Let us pray:
# Prayer # 1 – 1 Timothy 1:1 – 2:6

I thank you Jesus that You are my hope. I thank you for grace, mercy and peace which come from God our Father.

Lord may I exercise charity out of a pure heart and a good conscience, and faith that is unfeigned. Thank you Lord for enabling me and counting me faithful and putting me into ministry. I Thank you for Your mercy and for Your grace. Jesus, I thank you for coming into the world to save sinners of whom I am chief. Unto you O God, the King eternal, immortal, invisible, the only wise God; be honor and glory forever and ever.

Father, help me to walk in faith and with a good conscience. Holy Spirit, help me to offer supplications, prayers, intercessions and the giving of thanks for all men; for kings and for all in authority; because this is good and acceptable in the sight of God. I pray that all kings, rulers, leaders and men everywhere, will be saved and be brought into the knowledge of the truth. There is only one God and one mediator between God and men, the man Christ Jesus. I thank you Jesus for giving Yourself a ransom for all. Amen!

# Prayer # 2 – 1 Timothy 2:9 – 6:19

**For women**: Lord, help me as a woman to adorn myself with good works and not to usurp authority over men. Help me Holy Spirit to continue in faith, charity, holiness and sobriety.

Lord may our leaders be vigilant, sober, of good behavior, given to hospitality, apt to teach, not given to wine, not guilty of filthy lucre but patient; not a brawler, not covetous but rule their household well.

Let our leaders, O Lord, hold the mystery of the faith in a pure conscience. Help us O Lord to exercise ourselves unto godliness; godliness Your Word says is profitable unto all things.

Father guard my heart from falling away from following You. Some will depart from the faith, giving heed to seducing spirits and doctrines of devils. Guard my heart from these.

Lord I pray for our youths that no one will despise them, but they will be an example of the believers in word, in conversation, in charity, in spirit, in faith, and in purity.

Holy Spirit, help me to be contented because godliness with contentment is great gain. Guard my heart from the love of money. Father I choose to follow after righteousness, godliness, faith, love, patience, meekness. I will fight the good fight of faith. I lay hold on eternal life.

Lord you are the only Potentate, the King of kings and Lord of lords. To You be honor and power everlasting.

Lord, I pray for those who are rich in this world that they be not high minded or trust in uncertain riches but in the living God who gives us richly all things to enjoy. I pray Father that they will do good and be rich in good works, ready to distribute and willing to communicate; laying up in store for themselves a good foundation against the time to come that they may lay hold on eternal life. In Jesus' name I pray. Amen!

*Praying*

# 11 Timothy

## Summary of the book

In the book of Second Timothy Paul wrote his final thoughts to his son, Timothy. Within its pages, Paul continues to offer encouragement to Timothy in the work of His ministry.

As you pray Second Timothy, you will pray the last words of a great man of God. His last words to Timothy and everyone who will claim to follow Christ.

## Let us pray:
## Prayer # 1 – 11 Timothy 1:3 – 4:8

Holy Spirit, help me to stir up the gift that is within me. Remove from me fear, for God has not given me a spirit of fear but of power, and of love, and of a sound mind. Father, I am not ashamed of the testimony of our Lord. Thank you Father for saving me and calling me with a Holy calling, according to Your own purpose and grace, which was given to me in Christ Jesus, before the world began.

Lord I believe in You, and I know that You are able to keep that which I have committed unto You against that day. I will hold fast, the form of sound words in faith and love, in Christ Jesus.

Lord, I declare that I am strong in the grace that is in Christ Jesus. Help me to endure hardship as a good soldier of Jesus Christ. Help me Holy Spirit, not to entangle myself with the affairs of this life but to please you in everything. I am dead with Christ and shall also live with Him. If I suffer with Him, I shall also reign with Him.

Help me Holy Spirit to study to show myself approved unto God, a workman not ashamed but rightly dividing the word of truth. Lord I shun profane and vain babbling. Lord I want to be a vessel unto honor, sanctified and meet for Your use and to be prepared unto every good work.

I flee all youthful lusts and I follow righteousness, faith, charity and peace. Help me Holy Spirit to be gentle unto all men; apt to teach and patient.

Holy Spirit, help me to continue in things which I have been taught in the Scriptures which is able to make me wise through faith which is in Christ Jesus. Your Word O God is profitable for doctrine, for reproof, for correction, for instruction in righteousness. Let these help me to be thoroughly furnished unto all good works.

Let me preach the Word in season and out of season; reproving, rebuking and exhorting with all longsuffering and doctrine. Help me to watch thou in all things and endure afflictions, do the work of an evangelist and make full proof of my ministry.

Lord, at the end of my journey, cause me to be able to say like Paul, I have fought a good fight, I have finished my course, I have kept the faith, and laid up for me, will be a crown of righteousness which the Lord, the righteous Judge, shall give unto me, at that day. In Jesus name I pray, Amen.

*Praying*

# Titus

## Summary of the book

Similar to First and Second Timothy, the author wrote this book to offer encouragement and instruction to Titus, a leader in the church. The book of Titus shows the organization and life of the early church. Written in the pages are principles for structuring churches and instructions in becoming responsible leaders.

As you pray Titus, you will pray for your church's leadership and for right living in the church and in society.

# Prayer #1 – Titus 1:2 – 3:6 (AMP)

Thank you Father for the hope of eternal life that you have promised before the world began. You are faithful to Your promise because You are the God who cannot lie.

Father, I pray for the leaders of the church: pastors, elders, bishops, deacons; that they be blameless, faithful to their spouses, and raising disciplined children. I pray that our leaders will be blameless as stewards of God. They will not be self-willed or arrogant; they will not be quick-tempered or angry, or given to drink or violence. Help them Holy Spirit, not to be greedy for filthy lucre or financial gain. Help them instead, to be lovers of hospitality, lovers of goodness, of good people, and good things; sober-minded, upright and fair-minded; just, holy and temperate. Help our leaders Holy Spirit, to hold fast to the faithful words they have been taught; that they may be able to exhort and instruct those who contradict and oppose sound doctrine.

Let our older men be sober, grave, temperate, sound in faith, in charity and patience. Let our older women be reverent and devout in their behavior; not slanderers or false accusers; not given to much wine but be teachers of good things. Let them teach the younger women to be sober; to love their husbands and to love their children; to be discreet, chasten, homemakers, good-natured; submitting to their husbands that they bring no reproach to the Word of God.

Help our young men also, to be sober-minded. Let them show themselves in all things, to be a pattern of good works, in doctrine, showing in-corruptness, gravity, sincerity and sound speech.

Help those of us who serve to be obedient to our leaders.

We are no longer slave to sin or to any man but we are servants of Christ. Help me to be obedient to Christ and to please Him well in all things. Father I deny and reject ungodliness and worldly lust, and I choose to live soberly, righteously and godly in this present world. I look for that blessed hope and the glorious appearing of our God and our Savior Jesus Christ. I thank you Jesus for giving Yourself for us and for redeeming us from all iniquity and purifying us unto Yourself, a peculiar people who are zealous of good works.

Help me God, to submit to leaders and authorities; to be obedient and willing to do any good work. Sanctify my tongue that I speak evil of no man; to slander or abuse anyone. Help me to avoid being brawling or contentious but to be gentle and forbearing, and show meekness to all men.

Thank you Lord that by Your mercy, You have saved me, not by works of my own righteousness but by the washing/cleansing of the new birth (regeneration) and the renewing of the Holy Ghost, which You have poured out so richly upon me, through Jesus Christ my Savior. Being justified by Your grace, I am made heir according to the hope of eternal life.

Father, help us who have believed in You to apply ourselves to honorable occupations and to doing good. Help us to avoid stupid and foolish controversies about the law for they are unprofitable and futile.

To You father I give all the glory, the honor and Praise in Jesus name, Amen!

# General Epistles:

*Praying*

# Hebrews

### Summary of the book

The book of Hebrews was written to highlight Christ's superiority over Judaism. The message of Hebrews is that Jesus is better, Christianity is superior and Christ is sufficient for salvation. In the book we see Christ superiority over angels, over Old Testament leaders and priests. Christianity offers us a better covenant, a better sanctuary and a more sufficient sacrifice for sins through Christ Jesus.

As you pray Hebrews, you are confirming the superiority of Jesus Christ and your commitment to living by faith in Christ Jesus.

# Prayer # 1 – Hebrews 1:1 – 6:12 (AMP)

Father I thank you for speaking to us by Your Son, whom You have appointed heir of all things and by whom also You made the worlds. He is the brightness of Your glory and the express image of Your person and upholding all things by the word of His power; who having purged our sins is now sitting down on the right hand of the Majesty on high.

Jesus Christ has been made so much better than the angels, and His throne is forever and ever, and the scepter of His Kingdom is a scepter of absolute righteousness. You have loved righteousness and You have hated lawlessness. Therefore God, even Your God has anointed You with the oil of exultant joy and gladness above and beyond Your companions.

Lord, You did lay the foundation of the earth in the beginning and the heavens are the works of Your hands. They will perish but You remain and continue permanently. You remain the same and Your years will never end nor come to failure.

Christ Jesus, You are preeminent. All things have been put in subjection under You. You are crowned with glory and honor and by the grace of God, have tasted death for every man; to make the captain of our salvation perfect through sufferings and through death. You have destroyed him whom had the power of death, that is, the devil.

I thank you Jesus that by Your death, You have brought the devil to nothing and made him of no effect. Thank you for delivering and completely setting free all those who through the fear of death, were held in bondage. I thank you Jesus that You are a merciful and faithful High Priest who has made atonement and propitiation for our sins.

Lord Jesus, You are the Apostle and High Priest of our

profession and faithful Son over Your house as Moses was faithful in his entire house. You are counted worthy of more glory than Moses, because he, who builds the house, has more glory than the house, and all that is built, is by God. Moses was faithful in all His house as a servant but You Christ, is faithful over Your house as a Son; whose house we are, if we hold fast to the confidence and the rejoicing of the hope, firm to the end. (KJV)

Holy Spirit, take away from me any wicked unbelieving heart that will lead me away from the living God. Help me Lord never to harden my heart to your voice but to keep it soft and responsive when you speak. Remove unbelief from me. Help me Father to be zealous to strive diligently to enter the rest of God. May your Word that is alive and full of power, sharper than any two-edged sword; able to divide soul and spirit and judges the thoughts and purposes of the heart, keep me in tuned to your will and purposes.

I thank you Jesus that You are my great High Priest, who is able to understand and sympathize with my weaknesses and infirmities. I draw near to Your throne of grace that I may receive mercy for my failures, and find grace to help me in every need.

Lord Jesus, You are called of God a High Priest after the order of Melchizedek, being made perfect, You became the author of eternal salvation unto all them that obey You.

Lord, You are the author and source of eternal salvation, to all those who give heed and obey You. Lord, help me to become experienced and skilled in the doctrine of righteousness.

Holy Spirit, help me not to grow disinterested and become spiritual sluggard. Help me instead to practice patient endurance, waiting for the promise. In Jesus' name, Amen!

# Prayer # 2 - Hebrews 7:1 - 13:21 (AMP)

You are, O Lord, a Priest forever according to the order of Melchizedek. You live on forever, always living to make petition to God and intercession for us. You are holy, blameless, unstained by sin, separated from sinners and exalted higher than the heavens.

Lord, imprint Your words upon my mind, my innermost thoughts and understanding. Engrave them upon my heart. Lord, I want You and no one else to be my God. Bring me O God into the new covenant of Your love.

I thank you Lord for being merciful and gracious towards my sin and forgetting my deeds of unrighteousness. I thank you that You are the negotiator and mediator of a new covenant and because of Your single offering for my sins; I am forever completely cleansed and made holy. I thank you Jesus for granting me full freedom and the confidence to enter into the Holy of holies by the power and virtue in Your shed blood.

Help me Holy Spirit not to fling away my fearless confidence. Grant me steadfast, patience and endurance to perform and fully accomplish the will of God, and thus receive what is promised. Help me to live by faith and not to shrink in fear.

Help me Father, to consider my brethren, to provoke unto love and good will. Help me not to forsake the assembling of ourselves but to be diligent in exhorting each other. Guard my heart from sinning willfully after receiving the knowledge of the truth. I will not cast away my confidence which has recompense of reward. The just shall live by faith. I choose Father, to live by faith. ( KJV)

Father God, I believe that You are God and that You are a rewarder of those who diligently seek You. I believe in You. I believe in Your Word. I believe in Your Son Jesus Christ and I believe in the Holy Spirit

Father, faith is the substance of the things we hope for and the evidence for the things we do not see. I thank you Father for the great cloud of witnesses of faith. It was by faith that they were able to obtain the promise. Help me to strip off and throw aside every encumbrance and sin that easily besets me and let me run with patient endurance the appointed course that is set before me. I focus my attention on Jesus, the author and finisher of my faith, who for the joy that was set before Him, endured the cross; despising its shame and is now seated at the right hand of throne of God. Father, turn me away from all that will distract me from Jesus. Bring my faith into maturity and perfection.

I thank you Lord, for loving me enough to correct and discipline me. Help me to receive Your correction as a reminder of Your love and Your acceptance, and the fact that You deal with me as Your beloved child.

Help me Holy Spirit to live in peace with everyone and to pursue that consecration and holiness without which no one will ever see the Lord. Help me to exercise foresight and to look after others, to see that no one falls back from and fail to secure God's grace. Help me to offer to God pleasing service and acceptable worship, with modesty and pious care, and godly fear and awe. Help me to love my fellow believers. Let my character be free from love of money and let me be satisfied with my present circumstances, and with what I have.

Lord, You Yourself have said, You will not in any way fail me nor give up on me nor leave me without support. You will not, You said, in any degree, leave me helpless nor forsake me, nor let me down, and for that I confidently say, the Lord is my Helper, I will not be seized with alarm. I will not fear or dread or be terrified.

Jesus Christ, You are the same yesterday, today and for-ever. The God of peace; the great Shepherd of the sheep; may you strengthen and make me what I ought to be, and equip me with everything good that I may carry out Your will. Work in me O God to accomplish that which is pleasing in Your sight through Jesus Christ. To You be glory forever and ever, Amen!

*Praying*

# James

### Summary of the book

The book of James comprises teachings on the ethical issues of the Christian life. There is a great admonition to the believer to put outward actions to their inward faith else their faith will do nothing. "Faith without works is dead." There is also admonition to seek after God's wisdom and be doers of the Word, not just hearers. The book of James gives a summary of how to live an effective Christian life.

Are you struggling with your faith? Do you have problems facing the trials and temptations of this life? Do you have a struggle to control your speech or do you lack genuine wisdom? As you pray the book of James you will gain victory over these struggles as you affirm the Word of God over your own life. You will allow the Word to produce within your Christian life, genuine faith, genuine wisdom, careful speech and contrite submission

# Prayer # 1 – James 1:2 – 5:16

God and Father of our Lord Jesus Christ, to You I give all the glory and the praise. Lord in You I rejoice. Help me Holy Spirit, to always be joyful when I face the trials of this life, knowing that trials will produce patience within me. Help me to allow patience to have its work that I may become perfect and complete, lacking nothing.

Lord in faith, I ask for more wisdom. Remove from me any form of double mindedness or unbelief, because a double minded man is unstable in all his ways.

Help me to endure temptation so that I will be able to receive the crown of life which you have promise to those who love You. Lord, cleanse me from every evil desire or lust that will cause me to be drawn away and sin against You, and produce within me death. Lord, where I have erred, please forgive me. Lord I want to be a kind of first fruits of Your creatures.

Help me Holy Spirit, to be swift to hear, slow to speak and slow to wrath; for wrath does not produce the righteousness of God. Lord I lay aside all filthiness and overflow of wickedness and I receive with meekness the engrafted Word which is able to save my soul. I want to be a doer of the Word and not only a hearer; so that I will not be deceived but be blessed in what I do.

Help me Holy Spirit to bridle my tongue; to visit orphans and widows when they are in trouble and to keep myself unspotted from the world. This is pure and undefiled religion in Your sight.

Lord, forgive me for the times I have shown partiality between the poor and the rich. I have sinned, by so doing; becoming a transgressor of the law. For this Lord, I ask Your forgiveness. Help me to be merciful to others.

Father, Your Word says, faith without works is dead; so help me to demonstrate my faith by my works. Cause faith to be made perfect by my works. Oh Lord, may I be justified by my works as Abraham and Rahab were justified by their works. For as the body without the spirit is dead so faith without works is dead.

Lord, forgive me for times I have offended with the words from my mouth. Help me Holy Spirit not to stumble in word, by controlling my tongue. Let the words from my tongue be words of blessing and not cursing.

Lord, may I walk in the wisdom that is from above, which is pure, peaceable, gentle, willing to yield, full of mercy and good fruits, without partiality and without hypocrisy. May I make peace and be at peace so that the fruits of righteousness can be sown in peace.

Father, deliver me from the desires for pleasure that war in my members. Remove from me lust, covetousness and prayerlessness. You said I do not have because I asked not. Lord where I have asked amiss, forgive me. Remove from me any friendship with the things of the world; friendship with the world is enmity with God. Lord, grant me grace as I humble myself to You.

Lord, I submit to You and I resist the devil in my life. As I draw near to You God, please draw near to me. Cleanse my hands and purify my heart. May You lift me up Father, as I humble myself before You.

Help me Holy Spirit, not to speak evil of others. Where I have judged others, I ask for Your forgiveness. Lord, help me to do the good that I know. Remove boasting of tomorrow from me. Let the Lord's will done in all I set out to do.

Father, I cry woe unto the rich man who lives on the

earth in pleasure and luxury, and who condemns and murders the just.

Help me to be patient in suffering as the prophets of old were. Remove far from me grumbling against others and swearing. Lord, You are compassionate and merciful. Let my yes be yes and my no, be no.

Lord, let the prayer of faith heal those who are sick. Let those who are suffering pray. Lord, Your Word says the power of faith shall save the sick and You shall raise him up and if he has committed any sin, they shall be forgiven him. Let the Elders of the church pray over those who are sick, anointing them with oil, in the name of the Lord, and they shall be healed. May our prayers be effective and fervent. Let those who are merry sing psalms unto You. In Jesus name I pray Amen!

*Praying*

# I Peter

## Summary of the Book

The book of First Peter was written when the church was undergoing extensive persecution. It offers encouragement to believers on living their Christianity amid suffering and preparing for difficulties. The author, Apostle Peter instructs on how trial refine one's faith; that in difficult times, Christians should live above reproach and be imitators of Christ. In the book, we find a call to holy living, to reverence and trust in God, to be honest and loving, and to become more like Christ.

As you pray these truths over your life, you are giving the Holy Spirit latitude to bring you into Christ's perfection; opening the door of God's blessings and a victorious Christian walk amid persecution.

### Let us pray:
# Prayer # 1 – 1 Peter 1:2 – 2:23 (AMP)

I thank you God my Father, for choosing me and conse-crating me by the Holy Spirit to be obedient to Jesus Christ, and to be sprinkled with His blood. Lord I pray that grace and peace be given unto me in increasing abundance.

All praise be to You God and Father of our Lord Jesus Christ, the Messiah. Lord by Your boundless mercy, I have been born anew into an inheritance beyond the reach of change and decay; reserved in heaven for me. I am being guarded by God's power through my faith until I fully inherit the salvation that is ready to be revealed in the last days. On this account Holy Spirit, help me to be exceedingly glad, though for a little while I might be distressed by trails and suffer temptations; so that the genuineness of my faith may be tested, which will resound to praise and glory and honor when Jesus Christ is revealed.

Lord, I love You and I believe in You, without having seeing You. Lord I set my hope wholly and unchangeable on the grace that will come to me when Jesus Christ the Messiah is revealed.

Lord I will walk in obedience. I will no longer conform myself to the evil desires that governed me whilst in my for-mer ignorance. But I choose to be, and set apart myself to be holy in all conduct, and manner of living. Holy Spirit, help me to conduct myself with true reverence throughout my time of temporary residence on earth, whether long or short.

Lord, I recognize and acknowledge that I have been re-deemed and ransomed from the useless/fruitless way of living inherited by tradition from our forefathers, not with corrupt-ible things such as silver and gold, but purchased with the pre-cious blood of Christ.

Through You Jesus, I have believed on God, and my hope is centered on Him. Jesus You are clothed with honor and with glory, given to You by the Father when He raised You from the dead.

Holy Spirit, help me to be obedient to the truth and purify my heart for the sincere affection of the brethren that I may love others fervently from a pure heart.

Thank you Father that I have been born again by the ever living and lasting Word of God; the Word, the gospel that endures forever. Let this Word, the good news, continues to be preached to others.

Lord, I put away every trace of wickedness and all deceit and insincerity, pretense and hypocrisy; grudges, envy and jealousy; slander and evil speaking of every kind. Instead I crave, thirst for; earnestly desire the pure unadulterated spiritual milk that by it, I may be nurtured and grow unto Salvation.

Lord, I come to You, the living stone which is chosen and precious in God's sight. Lord, may I like a living stone be built up into a spiritual house, holy, dedicated, consecrated; to offer up spiritual sacrifices that are acceptable and pleasing to You. Lord, help me never to be disappointed or ashamed, for I believe in the precious Chief Cornerstone, who is Jesus Christ, the Messiah.

I confess that I am among God's chosen race, a royal priesthood, a dedicated nation. I am God's own purchased special possession; to set forth the wonderful deeds and display the virtues and perfections of God who called me out of darkness into His marvelous light.

I thank you Lord that once we were not a people but now we are God's people. Once we were unpitied but now we are pitied and have received mercy.

Father, I commit to abstain from the sensual urges, the evil desires, and the passions of the flesh that wage war against my soul. I will conduct myself properly, honorably and righteously among others. Lord may others glorify You, having witness my good deeds.

Lord, I will submit to every human institution and authority for Your name sake. Where I have failed to do so, forgive me. Help me Lord to do what is right. Lord it is Your intention and will that by doing right, my good and honest life will silence the ignorant charges and ill-informed criticisms of foolish persons.

Help me Holy Spirit to live at all times as a servant of God. Let me not employ my freedom as a pretext for wickedness. Help me to show respect for all men; treating them honorably. Help me to love the brethren. Help me to reverence God and honor my leaders. Help me Father to be submissive to my leaders, with all proper respect; not only to those who are kind but those who are overbearing, unjust and crooked. Help me Holy Spirit to endure the pain of unjust suffering. May I follow in the steps of Christ who suffered for me, though He was guilty of no sin, neither was deceit ever found on His lips. When He was reviled and insulted, He did nor reviled or offer insult in return. When He was abused and suffered, he made no threat but trusted himself and everything to Him who judges fairly. Amen!

# Prayer #2 - 1 Peter 2:24 – 4:19 (AMP)

I thank you Christ for personally bearing my sins in Your body on the tree that I might die to sin and live to righteousness. Thank you Lord that by Your wounds I have been healed. Thank You for being the guardian and Bishop of my soul.

Lord I pray for wives that they be submissive to their husbands, so that even if any do not obey the Word of God, they may be won over; not by discussions but by the godly lives of their wives. Help wives O Lord, to conduct themselves in a pure and modest way; to reverence their husbands, to respect them, to honor, esteem, appreciate and adore them; to be devoted to them; to deeply love and enjoy their husbands. Let them win over their husbands not with external adorning but with the inward adorning and beauty of the hidden person of the heart, with the incorruptible and unfolding charm of a gentle and peaceful spirit.

Lord, I pray for the married men that they live considerately with their wives; honoring their wives as physically the weaker but at the same time realizing that they are joint heirs of the grace of life, so that their prayers be not hindered.

Help us Father, as Christian brethren to be of the same mind, united in spirit, sympathizing with each other; loving each other as brethren of one household, compassionate, courteous, tender-hearted, and humble.

Lord, when I am confronted with evil or insult, help me not to return same but instead blessing; praying for their welfare, happiness and protection and truly loving them. To this O God, I have been called.

Lord I want to enjoy and see good days, so help me to keep my tongue from evil and my lips from guile. Lord, I will turn away from wickedness and shun it. I will do right. I will search for peace and seek it eagerly with God, my fellowmen and myself.

Lord, let your eyes be upon me and let Your ears be open to my prayers. Lord, I set Christ as Holy in my heart and I acknowledge Him as Savior. Help me Holy Spirit to courteously and respectfully give an account of the hope that is in me to anyone who asks me.

I thank you Jesus for dying for my sins once and for all that You might bring me to God. Lord in Your human body, You were put to death but You were made alive in the Spirit. Lord, help me to patiently suffer for Christ rather than fail to please God.

Father, I choose not to spend the rest of my natural life living by human appetites and desires but I choose to live for what You will. Help me Holy Spirit to be sound-minded and self-restrained, and alert unto prayer. Give me an intense and unfailing love for the brethren. Help me to forgive and disregard the offenses of others because love covers a multitude of sin. Lord, help me to be hospitable. May I use my gifts faithfully.

Lord, I pray for those who have the gift of speech that they will speak as the oracle of God. Those who have the gift of service, will serve with the strength which God furnishes abundantly; so that in all things God may be glorified through Jesus Christ.

Lord may I rejoice despite sufferings, so that I can rejoice in triumph, when Your glory is revealed. Amen!

# Prayer # 3 – 1 Peter 5:1 – 10 (AMP)

Lord I pray for pastors, elders and spiritual guides of the Church that they will tend, nurture, guard, guide and fold the flock of God; not by coercion or constraint but willingly; not dishonorably, motivated by the advantages and profits belonging to the office but eagerly and cheerfully. Father, Let them not be domineering over those in their charge but being examples to the congregation. May they win the conquerors crown of glory when Christ is revealed. Help us as members of the congregation to be subject to the ministers and spiritual guides of the Church; giving them due respect and yielding to their counsel. Help us Father to walk in humility toward each other. Lord you set Yourself against the proud, the insolent, the overbearing, the disdainful, the presumptuous and the boastful but You give grace to the humble. Lord I humble myself under the mighty hand of God that in due time You will exalt me. I cast all my anxieties, my worries, my concerns on You Lord, for I know that You care for me.

Help me Holy Father to be well balanced, temperate and sober of mind. Lord, help me also to be vigilant and cautious at all times. Lord I stand firm against the devil in my life and Christian walk. I will remain firm in faith against all onsets. I will remain rooted, established, strong, immovable and determined.

Lord, I thank you that after I have suffered a little, the God of all grace, who imparts all blessings and favor and who has called me to His own eternal glory in Christ Jesus, will himself complete and make me what I ought to be; established and grounded securely.

To You O Lord I ascribe dominion, power and authority forever and ever. Amen

*Praying*

# 11 Peter

### Summary of Book

The book of Second Peter provides warning to the Christian believers of false teachers and encourages believers to grow in their knowledge of Jesus Christ. Similar to the early Christians we see false teachers around us, who tries to dispute the teachings of Christ. We see them every day on our televisions and radio programs.

As you pray Second Peter, you will reinforce and hold fast to your faith in Christ Jesus and His teachings; rejecting lies and false teachers.

# Prayer # 1 – 11 Peter 1:3 – 3:18 (AMP)

I thank you Father that Your divine power has bestowed upon me, all things that are suited to life and godliness, through my knowledge of Christ, who has called me by and to His own glory and excellence. Thank you also for bestowing on me, Your precious and exceedingly great promises; so that through them I may escape the moral decay that is in the world, because of covetousness. I thank you Lord for making me a partaker of the divine nature.

Help me Holy Spirit to add diligence to the divine promises, by employing every effort in exercising faith, to develop virtue. In exercising virtue, develop knowledge and in exercising knowledge develop self-control. In exercising self-control, develop steadfastness and in exercising steadfastness, develop godliness. In exercising godliness, develop brotherly affection and in exercising brotherly affection, develop Christian love. Father, let these qualities increasingly abound in me, so that I will not be idle or unfruitful in the knowledge of our Lord Jesus Christ.

Help me Holy Spirit to make sure my calling, an election, so that I will not stumble.

Lord, guard me from false prophets and false teachers. Rescue me O Lord out of temptations and trials. Lord, help me never to be made inferior or worse, or to be overcome by anything, thereby being enslaved by it.

Lord, I thank you that You do not delay nor are You tardy or slow about what You promise, accordingly to some people's conception of slowness. You are long suffering towards us. You do not desire that any should perish but that all should turn to repentance.

Lord, as I wait and earnestly long for the coming of the day of God, may I be found without spot or blemish and at peace. Help me Father to be on my guard, lest I be carried away by the error of lawlessness. Help me to grow in grace, and knowledge and understanding, of our Lord and Savior Jesus Christ. To You Lord we ascribe glory, honor, majesty and splendor, both now and to the day of eternity. In Jesus' name Amen!

*Praying*

# 1, 11 and 111 John

### Summary of books

The first epistle of John highlights for the reader, the important truth that God is Light; God is Love and God is Life. It explains to the reader the distinction between truth and error. As believers, we are brought into fellowship with God who is love and light and have the promise of eternal life through Jesus Christ. In the second epistle, 11 John, the reader is encouraged to continue in the truth by walking in love and avoiding error. There are those who teach otherwise, and John in his epistles refuted the errors of the false teachers. The third epistle, 111 John, the author, encourages us to give and to serve others as demonstration of our love.

## Let us pray:
# Prayer # 1 – 1 John 1:1 – 2:17

Father, You were from beginning, the Word of life, and our fellowship is with You, and Your Son Jesus Christ, our Savior.

Lord I confess that You are light and in You there is no darkness. I choose to walk in the light because You are in the light. Let the blood of Jesus cleanse me from all my sins. Lord ,I confess all my sins, and I ask that You forgive me of them all. Lord, You said if I confess my sin, You who are faithful and just, will forgive me and cleanse me, from all unrighteousness. Lord I confess of (confess all known sins). Please forgive me and cleanse me.

I thank you Jesus that You are the propitiation for our sins, and the sins of the whole world.

Holy Spirit, help me to abide in Christ, so as to walk, as He walked. Help me to keep His Word, so that the love of God is perfected in me. Lord, if there is any form of hatred in me, towards my brethren, forgive me, and deliver me. Lord, I want to love my brethren so that I will walk in light, and have no occasion of stumbling within me. Father, I confess that I am in the light and I will love my brethren.

I thank you Father that my sins are forgiven, for Christ name sake. Thank you for making Christ known to me from the beginning. Lord, help our young men to be strong. Let the Word of God abide in them, so that they will be able to overcome the wicked one.

Father, deliver me from any love of the world; deliver me from all that is in the world, the lust of the flesh, the lust of the eyes, and the pride of life. Help me to do the will of God.

# Prayer # 2 – 1 John 2:18 – 3:24

Father, I acknowledge Jesus Christ as the Son of God, and I believe in Him. I thank you Father, for the promise of eternal life, given to those who remain in You. I thank You Lord for the anointing that abides within me; the anointing that teaches me all things. I promise Father, to abide in You, and in Your Word.

Thank you Father for the love You have bestowed upon me that I should be called a Son of God. Lord, I do not yet know what I shall be, but I do know that when You appear I shall be like You, and I shall see You as You are. Help me Holy Spirit to purify myself with this hope I have in Christ Jesus. I am forever grateful that Christ was manifested to take away my sins, and in Him there is no sin; so if I abide in Him I should not sin. Lord, I am also grateful that Christ was manifested to destroy the works of the devil, who causes me to sin. Destroy the works of the devil in my life, in the life of my family, and friends.

Lord, cause Your seed to remain in me that I cannot sin. Lord, I want to do what is righteous.

Lord, as You laid down Your life for me, help me to lay my life down for the brethren, by loving them. Help me Father, to love them, and to have compassion on them. Help me Father to love not only in word or tongue but to love in deed and truth.

I thank you Father that You are greater than my heart, and You know all things. Thank you for the confidence I have in Christ because my heart condemns me not.

Lord, help me to keep Your commandments and do those things which are pleasing in your sight; so that whatever I ask, I will receive of You.

I believe on the name of Your Son Jesus Christ and I will love the brethren. Lord, thank you for the Spirit You have given to me as proof that You abide in me. Amen!

# Prayer # 3 – 1 John 4:1 – 5:21

I declare that I am of God and have overcome the evil one. Greater is Christ who is in me than he that is in the world. Lord, I pray against the spirit of error in our world, and I pray that the spirit of truth will destroy its work.

Father, I thank you for manifesting Your love to me, by sending Your only begotten Son into the world that we might live through him. Lord, You loved me and You sent Your Son to be the propitiation for my sins. Lord because You loved, I choose to love others. Father, You said everyone that loves is born of God and knows God. I am born again in Christ Jesus and I know You Father, therefore will I love.

Lord, let Your love be perfected in me as I love others. Jesus Christ You are the Savior of the world. I confess that Jesus is the Son of God. Father, You are love, and everyone that dwells in love, dwells in You and You in Him. Father, as You are, may I be in this world.

I rebuke fear from my life, because there is no fear in love. Father You said, perfect love casts out fear. Cast away fear from my life so that I can be perfected in love. Father I choose to love because You first loved me.

I thank you Father, for my faith that has given me the victory, and causing me to overcome the world. I declare that I am an over comer because I believe that Jesus is the Son of God. Thank you Father that I have life because I have the Son of God.

I thank you Father, for the confidence I have in You, because I believe on the name of Your Son and whatever I ask of You, according to Your will, You will hear me. And because You hear me, whatever I ask, I know that I have the petitions that I desire of You.

Thank you Father, that because I am begotten of You, the wicked one cannot touch me. I thank you Christ for coming, and giving me understanding that I may know You, who is true. You are Eternal Life. Keep me free from idols I pray. Amen!

## II John

Father, help me to walk in truth and to love the brethren. I pray against deceivers, those who do not confess that Jesus Christ is Lord. Let believers hold unto what they have been taught. Help us to remain and abide in the doctrine of Christ.

## III John

Lord, let Your people prosper and be in health as their soul prospers. Let them walk in truth. May we stand up for the truth of the Word. Lord, may we be of help to others who are of the truth and to strangers. May we be fellow helpers of the truth. Help me Holy Spirit to do that which is good because he that doeth good is of God. In Jesus Name. Amen!

*Praying*

# Jude

### Summary of the Book

The book of Jude was written at a time, false teachers were increasing in the Church. The book offers instruction to the believers on defending the truth of the Good News; "contending for the faith," by rejecting lies and immoralities.

As you pray Jude, proclaim the truth and decide within yourself, to stand firm in your faith and defend the truth of God; at all cost possible.

**Let us pray:**
# Prayer # 1 – Jude 1 - 24

I thank you God my Father, for sanctifying me, and for preserving me in Jesus Christ. Thank you for calling me. Lord, help me as a believer, to earnestly contend for the faith. I rebuke those who are turning the grace of God into lasciviousness, and who are denying the only Lord God and our Lord Jesus Christ. I rebuke the ungodly, the murmurers, the complainers; those who walk after their own lusts, and those who speak swelling words; having men's person in admiration because of advantage.

Help me, O Lord, to build up myself in my most holy faith; praying always in the Holy Ghost. Help me, Father, to keep myself in the love of God; looking for the mercy of my Lord Jesus Christ unto eternal life. Help me, Lord, to have compassion on others, making a difference.

Lord, I am confident that You are able to keep me from falling, and to present me faultless before the presence of Your glory, with exceeding joy.

To You O God, the only wise God; our Savior, be all the glory and the majesty; all the dominion and the power, both now and ever. AMEN!

# Apocalyptic Book:

*Praying*

# Revelation

### Summary of Book:

The book of Revelation unveils to us the glory of Christ and future events. This book was written at a particular time in history when the church was undergoing persecution and difficulty. It gives the believer a sense of hope. Hope in the fact, the risen Savior, Jesus Christ will return, to justify the righteous, and judge the wicked. It provides warning to the churches.

As you pray the book of Revelation, let your hope be renewed, knowing that God is in control. Christ victory is assured and everyone who trusts in Him will be saved. By reading the book of Revelation, you are promised a blessing.

**Let us pray:**
# Prayer # 1 – Revelation 1:4 – 3:22

Lord I declare, You are He, Who is, and Who was, and Who is to come. I declare that Jesus Christ is the faithful witness, and the first begotten of the dead; the prince of the kings of the earth. I am loved of Him, and through His blood I am washed from all my sins. He has made us kings and priests to God. To Him, I give glory, and dominion forever. I declare that He shall come with the clouds and every eye shall see Him, and all kindred's of the earth shall wail because of Him. Lord, You are the Alpha and Omega; the beginning and the end; who is, who was, and the one, who is to come; the Almighty. You are the first and the last. You live forever and ever more. You, O Lord have the keys of hell and of death.

Forgive me Lord for leaving my first love. I repent and return to do the first works. Lord as promised to those who overcome, give to me to eat of the tree of life, which is in the midst of the paradise of God. Help me Holy Spirit to remain faithful, amid distress and poverty; even to death, that I may receive the crown of life, which the Father shall give to those who overcome. Help me to hold fast to Your name, O Lord, and not to deny the faith. Remove from me the worshipping of idols, and those who worship idols. Lord I want to eat of the hidden manna and receive a white stone with a new name written in it. Help me to overcome the evil around me.

Lord, Your eyes are likened to a flame of fire and Your feet are like fine brass. You search out the reins and heart, and give to everyone according to their works. Let my work be pure, Father. I thank you Lord, for the power You will give over the nations, to them who overcome. Lord let my ears be open to what the Spirit is saying to the Churches.

Lord, help me to be watchful, and to strengthen the things that remain that are ready to die. Lord, where You have not found my works to be perfect before God, please pardon me. Help me not to defile my garments, so I will walk with You in white, as worthy. O Lord, confess my name before the Father and His angels. Do not blot out my name, from the book of life.

Lord, You are holy and You are true. You have the key of David, and whatever You open, no one can shut, and whatever You shut, no one open. Let my ways please You, O Lord. Set before me an open door, where no one can shut. Lord I purpose in myself that though sometimes I might have little strength, I will keep thy Word and will not deny Your name. Keep me O Lord from the hour of temptation, as I keep thy Word.

Lord, You are the Amen, the faithful and true witness; the beginning of God's creation. I thank you that You rebuke me because You love me. Lord, please remove from me lukewarmness in my Christian walk; remove from me dependence on riches and material possessions. Let not my confidence rest in these but in You, Sovereign Lord. Grant me Your counsel that I may be rich in You, and be clothed in white garments; so my nakedness does not appear. Father I repent. Please come in, and sup with me, as I hear Your voice. Holy Spirit, help me to overcome, so that I can sit with the Father on His throne. O God, give me a listening ear, to hear what the Spirit is saying to the churches. Amen!

## Prayer # 2 – Revelation 5:19 – 18:4

Holy, Holy, Holy, Lord God Almighty, who was, and is, and is to come. To You, I give glory and honor, and thanks; who lives, forever and ever. You are worthy O Lord to receive glory, and honor, and power. For You have created all things and for thy pleasure, they are, and were created. You are the Lion of the tribe of Judah, the Root of David, who have prevailed to open the Book, and loosen the seven seals thereof. You alone are Worthy to take the Book and to open the seals thereof. For You were slain, and have redeemed us to God by Your blood; from every kindred, and tongue, and people, and nation; You have made us kings and priests, and we shall reign on earth. Worthy is the Lamb that was slain, to receive power and riches, and wisdom and strength, and honor and glory, and blessings. Blessings and honor, glory and power, to You who sits on the throne, and to the Lamb, forever and ever.

Lord, when the great day of Your wrath shall come, no one shall be able to stand.

O Father, I look forward with great expectation for the day, when all nations and kindred, and people and tongues, shall stand before Your throne, and before the Lamb, clothed in white robes and palms in our hands, crying with loud voices saying, "Salvation to our God which sits on the throne and to the Lamb". The angels, the elders, and the four beasts worshipping You saying; "Blessings and thanksgiving, and honor and power, and might, be to our God, forever and ever, amen."

Lord, I look forward to the day, when I shall serve You night and day in Your temple. I look forward to the day when I will hunger no more, nor thirst anymore because You O Lord, the Lamb in the midst of us, will feed us and lead us unto living fountains of waters, and God shall wipe away all tears from our eyes. Hallelujah.

Father, I look forward to the day when the kingdoms of this world will become the Kingdom of my Lord and of His Christ, and He shall reign forever and ever. I shall join the four and twenty elders worshipping, saying: 'We give thanks O Lord God Almighty which art and was and art to come; because Thou has taken thy great power and has reigned."

Lord, we rejoice for that day, when that old serpent, called the Devil and Satan, who deceives the whole world, will be cast out into the earth, along with his angels. In that day, Salvation and strength shall come and the Kingdom of our God and the power of His Christ; for the accuser of my brothers is cast down. I shall overcome by the blood of the Lamb and by the word of my testimony, and shall love not my life to death.

I thank you Lord, that my name is written in the Lamb's book of life, who is the foundation of the world. Father, the day will come when the saints shall sing great and marvelous are Your works, Lord God Almighty; just and true are Your ways, King of the saints. On that great day, who shall not fear You, O Lord, and glorify your name? For You are holy. All nations shall come, and worship before You, for Your judgments are shown.

Preserve me from the wrath to come on the earth, and its inhabitants. Let me be watchful and keep my garments, less I walk naked, and others see my shame.

Lord, the kings of the earth on that great day shall not prevail against You, instead the Lamb shall overcome them; for He is Lord of lords and King of kings, and they that will be with Him are called, and chosen, and faithful.

Father, guard my heart from becoming partaker of the sins of the earth, and from receiving of its plagues. Amen!

# Prayer # 3 – Revelation 19:1 – 22:21

Hallelujah, Salvation and Glory, and Honor, and Power, unto the Lord our God. True and Righteous are Your judgments. For You will judge the great whore which corrupts the earth with her fornication, and will avenge the blood of Your servants. Amen!

Hallelujah, for the Lord God, Omnipotent reigns. We will be glad and rejoice, and give honor to You Lord, for the marriage of the Lamb is come, and Your wife the church have made herself pure. Blessed are they which shall be called unto the marriage supper of the Lamb. Thank you Lord that the testimony of Jesus is the spirit of prophecy.

Lord Jesus, You are faithful and true, and in righteousness You judge and make war. Your eyes are as flame of fire. You are the Word of God, King of kings, and Lord of lords. You are the righteous judge.

Lord I pray for the New Jerusalem; the new heaven and the new earth, where the tabernacle of God will be with man. You will dwell with us and we shall be Your people, and God himself shall be with us, and be our God. O heavenly Father, I look forward to the day when You shall wipe away all tears from my eyes, and there shall be no more death, neither sorrow, nor crying, neither shall there be any more pain; for the former things shall pass away. Lord, You shall make all things new. You are the Alpha and Omega, the Beginning and the End. Lord, freely grant unto me, of the fountain of the water of life. Help me to overcome, so that I can inherit all things, and You shall be my God, and I shall be Your child. All fearful and unbelieving, abominable and murderers, whoremongers and sorcerers, idolaters and all liars, shall have their part in the lake, which burns with fire and brimstone.

Oh Lord, I pray for that great city, the Holy Jerusalem which shall descend out of heaven from God; having the Glory of God; whose walls shall be great and high; whose foundation will be garnished with all manner of precious stones, and the Lord God Almighty, and the Lamb, will be the temple of it. The Holy city that has no need for the sun, neither the moon to shine in it; for the Glory of God shall lighten it, and the Lamb shall be the light of it. All nations which are saved, shall walk in the light of it, and the kings of the earth, will bring their glory and honor into it.

God our Father and the precious Lamb, I look forward to seeing Your face, and having Your name on my forehead, in that Holy city, where the pure river of water of life, clear as crystal, proceeds out of it; from Your throne. There we will serve You Lord, as Your servants.

Come quickly Lord. You are the Alpha and Omega, the beginning and the end, the first and the Last. Lord, I will commit to do Your commandments, so that I may have right to the tree of life, and may enter in through the gates into the city. You are the root and the offspring of David, and the bright and morning star. Come quickly, even so, come Lord Jesus. Amen.

# Bonus Prayers:

# Deuteronomy

The God of our forefathers, Abraham, Isaac, Jacob and the promised seed, Jesus Christ our Savior, bless me a thousand times so much more as I am now.

Father, You are the Lord my God who goes before me, and fights for me. I will therefore not be afraid or discouraged in anything. Father, go before me and show me the way I should go. Grant unto me the faith and courage of Caleb.

Father, bless me in all the works of my hands. Cause me O Lord not to be in lack of nothing.

Father, I choose to walk in Your statutes and Your commandments. Let them be my wisdom and my understanding in the sight of others. Thank you Lord that You are nigh unto me. Thank you for Your righteous statutes and judgments. Help me Holy Spirit to take heed to myself and to keep my soul diligently, so that I will not forget the things which I have learnt. Help me to teach them to my children.

I thank you Father for being a merciful God. You will not forsake me nor will You destroy me; neither forsakes the covenant of our fathers which You swore unto them. Lord, I will seek You with all my heart. I will walk in obedience to Your commandments.

The Lord my God, You are God and there is no one else beside You. You are God in the heaven above and upon the earth beneath. Therefore I will keep Your commandments, so that it will go well with me, and with my children after me. Father all that You command that will I do. I will have no other god before You. I will not take the name of the Lord my God in vain. I will sanctify the Sabbath day to keep it holy. I will honor my father and my mother. I will not kill nor commit adultery; I will neither steal nor bear false witness; neither will I covet my neighbors' possession. Father, as it is summed up in the New Testament covenant, I will love You with all my heart, my mind, my soul and my strength and I will love my neighbors as myself.

Father, give me a heart that will fear You, and keep all your commandments always that it might be well with me, and with my children forever.

O Lord my God, You are one Lord. I will love You with all my heart and with all my soul and with all my might. The words that You teach me shall be in my heart and I will teach them diligently unto my children. I will talk of them when I sit in my house, and when I walk by the way; when I lie down and when I rise up. O Lord, let Your Word be as frontlets between my eyes. May I write them upon the post of my house, and on the gates.

Father, I want to walk in the blessings of Abraham, Isaac and Jacob. Grant unto me great and goodly cities which I did not build. Grant unto me houses full of all good things; vineyards and olive trees that I did not plant. Father when You bless me, help me to take heed, and beware lest I forget You. I choose O Lord to fear You and to serve You. I will diligently keep the commandments of the Lord my God, and His testimonies, and His statutes. I will do that which is right and good in the sight of the Lord. Help me Father to cast out all mine enemies from before me.

I thank you Father for loving me, and redeeming me out of the house of bondage. Lord, You are a faithful God who keeps covenant and mercy with them that love You, and keep Your commandments and repay them that hate You to their face, to destroy them. Thank you Father that when I hearken unto Your judgments, to keep and to do them, You will keep unto me the covenant and the mercy which you swore unto our fathers. You will love me and bless me, and multiply me. You will bless the fruit of my womb and the fruit of my land; my corn, my wine, and my oil. You will bless me above all people. You will take away all sickness, from me.

Father, I want to walk humbly before You and to keep Your commandments; to walk in Your ways and to fear You. I will remember thee, O Lord my God, for it is You who gives me power to get wealth. I choose O Lord, to walk in obedience and to obey the voice of the Lord.

Lord, You are the consuming fire, so go before me and destroy my enemies; bring them down before Your face. Help me to drive them out and to destroy them quickly. Lord, You require of me to fear You, to walk in all Your ways, to love You, and to serve You, with all my heart, and with all my soul; to keep Your commandments and statutes, and these will I do.

Father, the heaven, and the heaven of heavens, belongs to You; the earth also, with all that it consists. O Lord my God, You are God of gods, and Lord of lords; a great God, a mighty and terrible God, which regard not persons, nor take reward. Lord, you execute the judgment of the fatherless and widow, and love the stranger, in giving him food and raiment.

O Father may our country be a land which thou care for. Let Your eyes O Lord our God, be always upon it, from the beginning of the year, even unto the end of the year. Help us as a country to love You Lord our God, and to serve You with all our hearts, and with all our soul; so that we may receive rain on the land in its due season; the first rain and the latter rain; so that we may gather in corn, wine and oil. O God, send grass in our fields for our cattle.

Guard my heart God from being deceived to turn aside and serve other gods and worship them.

Help me Father to open mine hand wide open unto my brother, the poor and the needy. Let justice and righteous judgments be in our dealings with everyone.

Father, I will bring unto You the first fruit of all my labors which thou hast given unto me. I will set it before You Lord my God, and I will worship before You. I will rejoice in every good thing which the Lord my God has given unto me.

Lord, I will hearken to thy voice and will do all that thou has commanded me. Look down from thy holy habitation, from heaven, and bless thy people and the possessions thou have given us.

Father, today I commit to keep all Your statutes and judgments, to do them with all my heart and with all my soul. I pledge to walk in Your ways and to hearken to Your voice. You promised Lord that when we walk in obedience, You will set us high above all nations in praise and in name and in honor that we may be a holy people unto You, Lord our God.

Cause Your blessings, O God, to come upon me and overtake me. Bless me in the city and bless me in the field. Bless the fruit of my body, and the fruit of my ground. Bless my basket and my storehouse. Bless me when I come in, and when I go out. Father, cause my enemies that rise up against me, to be smitten before my face. Cause them to flee before me seven ways. Lord, command Your blessings upon my storehouses and in all that I set my hand to do. Bless me O Lord in this land. Establish us as a holy people unto yourself; so that all the people of the earth shall see that we are called by the name of the Lord.

Father, make me plenteous in goods, in the fruit of my

body and in the fruit of my ground. Open unto me O Lord your good treasure; the heaven to give the rain unto the land in its season. Father, Bless the work of my hand. Make me the head, and not the tail. Cause me to be above only, and not beneath. Lord, I will not go aside from any of the words which You have commanded me, to the right hand, or to the left; to go after other gods to serve them.

Lord, I will serve You with joyfulness, and with gladness of heart, for the abundance of all things. Father, rejoice over me to do me good, and to multiply me, and not to destroy me.

Holy Spirit, help me never to depart from following after God. Circumcise my heart to love the Lord my God with all mine heart, and with all my soul. Lord let the Word be nigh unto me, in my mouth, and in my heart, that I may obey to do it.

Lord, I choose life and goodness. I will love You and I will obey Your voice. I will cleave to You, for You are my life, and the length of my days. Lord I will be strong and of good courage. I will not fear or be afraid of my enemies. For You O Lord my God is He that goes with me, and You will not fail me nor forsake me. In Jesus name I pray, AMEN!

# Malachi

Father, I thank you for Your love. Forgive me, when I have questioned Your love for me.

Lord, I confess that You are my Father and my Master. Forgive me for times I did not honor you as Father, nor fear you as Master. Forgive me Lord for despising Your name. Forgive me for offering worship that was unacceptable; from polluted lip and heart; with the wrong attitude. Lord be merciful unto me and be gracious unto me.

Lord, from the rising of the sun to its setting, Your name shall be great among the nations, and in every place, worship shall be given to Your name. You are indeed a great King and Your name is terrible, and to be feared among the nations.

Forgive me, O Lord, for profaning Your name, by my actions and attitude to worship. Bring me into the fear of Your name. O God, my Father and Master, I will lay it to heart, to give glory and reverence to Your name.

I thank you Father, that Your covenant is one of life and peace, and in return, I am to revere You, and stand in awe of Your name. Lord may the law of truth be in my mouth; let not unrighteousness be on my lips. May I walk with You in peace and uprightness.

Lord, I pray for those entrusted as messengers of the Lord of hosts that their lips guard and keep pure the knowledge of Your Word and may others seek instruction at their mouth.

Lord I repent on behalf of those who have caused others to stumble. Forgive us for dealing faithlessly and treacherously against our brothers. May You accept our worship with favor.

Holy Spirit, help husbands to honor their marriage vows by not dealing treacherously and faithlessly to their wives. Lord you made the husband and the wife one flesh, so that godly offspring could be created from the union.

Lord, I come against divorce, separation and violence. Lord, You hate divorce and marital separation, and him who cover his wife with violence.

Thank you that the Messiah has come, Jesus Christ. We seek Him and we desire Him. Lord you are like a refiner's fire and like fullers' soap. Sit as a refiner and purifier of silver and purify me. Refine me O God like gold and silver that I may offer to the Lord offerings in righteousness.

Lord draw near to us for judgment. Be a swift witness against sorcerers, against adulterers; against false swearers; those who oppress the worker in his wages.

I thank you Lord that You do not change, and that is why, we are not consumed.

Lord, I choose to return to You with all my heart and with all my soul. Forgive me for robbing and defrauding You, by withholding my tithes and offerings. Forgive us as a people, and as a nation.

Father, I commit to bring all my tithes to the storehouse that there may be food in Your house. And as I do so, Open the windows of heaven and pour out a blessing that there shall not be room enough to receive it. Rebuke the devourer for my sakes. Let my possessions be a delight. Lord, I choose to reverenced and worshipfully fear You. I will think on Your name. You are my Lord and my God. I am Your special possession, Your peculiar treasure, Your jewel. Spare me O Father, as a man spares his own son, who serves him.

Help me Holy Spirit, to discern between the righteous and

the wicked, between him who serves God and him who does not serve Him.

Father, I thank you that the Sun of Righteousness has risen with healing in His wings, and His beams unto those who revere and fear His name. The lawless and wicked shall be ashes under the soles of our feet, because we will tread them down.

Father we earnestly hold onto Your words and will walk in them. In Jesus Name, Amen!

# Proverbs chapters 1- 9

Lord, pour out the Spirit of wisdom upon me and make me wise. Forgive me when wisdom called me so often but I didn't come; when wisdom reached out to me but I paid no attention. Forgive me, for the times I ignored and rejected the correction that wisdom offered. Lord I choose to listen to You. I choose knowledge and the fear of the Lord. Lord, I cry out for insight and understanding. O Lord, grant me wisdom. Grant unto me a treasure of good sense. Guard my path, and protect me Lord. Let wisdom enter my heart, and knowledge fill me with joy. Let wise planning O Lord, watch over me, and understanding keep me safe. Let wisdom save me from evil people and from those whose speech is corrupt.

Lord let wisdom save our young men from the immoral woman, from the flattery of the adulterous woman. Let them follow the steps of good men and stay on the paths of the righteous.

Lord, help me to store your commands in my heart. Help me to be loyal and kind. Let me be adorned with them, so that I can find favor with You and man, and be able to gain a good reputation. Lord I will trust You with all my heart, and will not depend on my own understanding. I will seek Your will in all I do. I choose O Lord the fear of the Lord and will turn my back on all evil. Help me Lord to be renewed in health and vitality, as I walk in the fear of the Lord.

Lord as I honor You with my wealth, and with the best part of everything; I pray that You will fill my life with riches, and may my storehouse overflow with the finest of things.

Father I thank you for Your corrections; may I never grow discouraged when You discipline me because you correct and discipline those whom You love. I thank you Father for loving me.

Lord, may I find wisdom and gain understanding. I desire wisdom more than rubies and gold. Let wisdom guide me down delightful paths. Lord, grant unto me out of Your rich treasure wisdom, understanding and knowledge. Lord, let me never lose sight of good planning and insight. Let them fill me with life, and bring me honor and respect. May they keep me safe on my way and keep my feet from stumbling. Lord, You are my security, and so I will not be afraid of disaster or destruction that comes upon the wicked. Keep my feet from being caught in a trap. Help me not to withhold good from those who deserve it, when it is in my power to help. Let me not plot against my neighbor who trusts me nor make accusations against someone who hasn't wronged me.

Lord, let your blessings be upon my home, as I walk uprightly before You. Lord, let me obtain favor from You as I walk humbly and inherit honor. Lord, help me to be wise and to develop good judgment. Let wisdom exalt me. Let wisdom honor me and present me with a beautiful crown, as I embrace her. Help me live a life guided by wisdom.

Lord, I will give attention to what You say. I will not lose sight of Your Word. Help me Holy Spirit to let them penetrate deep within my heart. As I discover the meaning in Your Word, may they bring me life and radiant health. Help me Holy Spirit to guard my heart, for it affects everything I do. I will avoid all perverse talk and I will stay away from corrupt speech. Holy Spirit, help me to look straight ahead, and to fix my eyes on what lies before me. Help me to mark out a straight path for my feet, and to stick to that path. Remove from me every distraction and keep my feet from following evil.

**(For wives)** Lord may I be a fountain of blessing for my husband. May he rejoice in me. May I be a loving doe and a graceful deer. Let my breast satisfy him always. Let my husband be always captivated by my love. Guard his heart, his mind and his eyes from the immoral woman. I declare over my husband that he will not be captivated by any immoral woman or embrace the breasts of any adulterous woman. He will be captivated only with my love and will be satisfied only with my breasts. Lord, examine every part that my husband takes. Let him not become captive by any sin; let him exercise self-control.

Lord, help me to be industrious and not a lazy body. Remove from me a haughty eye; a lying tongue; hands that kill the innocent; a heart that plots evil and feet that race to do wrong. Help me not to be a false witness who pours out lies or one who sows discord among others. These O God are detestable to You, let me not embrace any.

Lord I choose to follow Your advice. I will guard Your teaching as my most precious possession. Let me tie them on my fingers as a reminder and write them deep within my heart.

**(For wives)** Lord let my husband love wisdom like a sister and let him make insight a beloved member of the family so that he will be held back from an affair with an immoral woman and from listening to the flattery of an adulterous woman.

Help me Holy Spirit not to shut my ears or eyes to understanding or common sense. Lord, I desire the truth in everything. Keep my heart free from every kind of deception. Lord I seek your advice which is wholesome and good. Grant unto me good judgment, knowledge and discernment, good advice and success, insight and strength. Grant me wisdom O Lord I pray. Let wisdom fill my treasuries with gifts that are better than the purest gold and wages better than sterling silver.

O God my cry is for wisdom, for those who find her, finds life, and wins approval from the Lord. AMEN!

# PRAYER JOURNAL

Situation/Problem:

Scriptural support:

Personalized Prayer (write out your request)

Answer (answer from God)

# PRAYER JOURNAL

Situation/Problem:

Scriptural support:

Personalized Prayer (write out your request)

Answer (answer from God)

# PRAYER JOURNAL

Situation/Problem:

Scriptural support:

Personalized Prayer (write out your request)

Answer (answer from God)

# PRAYER JOURNAL

Situation/Problem:

Scriptural support:

Personalized Prayer (write out your request)

Answer (answer from God)

CPSIA information can be obtained
at www.ICGtesting.com
Printed in the USA
BVOW08s2059080617

486265BV00001B/65/P

9 781478 755999